MOBILE MARKETING

Dr JAMES SELIGMAN

Table of Contents

PRELUDE

The world is full of mobile devices as our lifestyles convert to more mobility and desire for access to information 24/7 at any time of day. Being connected is the new safety blanket of modern society as we eat, sleep, work, relax with our closest friend close at hand, the mobile device.

To be connected is to belong in today's millennial driven marketplace, where experiences are more valuable than buying goods or services. The desire for instant access, self-gratification, sharing our message or 'selfie' on the spot is the basis of this mobile phenomena.

How do marketers address this mobile community has become a powerful debate amongst scholars and practitioners?

By evaluating research, one is compelled to appreciate how mobile devices have become a critical communication device used in mass, that allow delivery and two-way exchange far beyond the capability of established media such as television, radio or press.

The conclusion is simple enough, no longer can marketing teams ignore mobile marketing. It has become a critical pillar in the strategy of marketing communications, it can no longer be ignored.

AUTHOR BIO

James Seligman was the Director responsible for the Masters in Marketing Management at the School of Management, Faculty of Management and Law, University of Southampton. An innovative 12-month international program, which uses the new DNA model of marketing theory and practice modules developed by the Marketing subject group. He joined Southampton University in 2008 and retired in late 2015. The MSc in Marketing Management degree has wide commercial support as it produces students who are trained for today's marketing challenges and considers technology as an enabler in modern marketing.

He has a Masters in Marketing and three undergraduate degrees in Business Administration, Educational Studies, and Psychology. His PhD is on Customer Experience and Technology and Digital Technology in Marketing.

As a Principal Fellow, he was also engaged in educational development and the student experience. The author of several books and journal articles, James research interests lie in the marketing of education, CRM and CEM, as well as the wider marketing characteristics of Brand, Strategic Marketing Intelligence, Analytics, Integrated Marketing Communications, Value Propositions, and Customer Insight. His most recent research has been on CEM and technology, Artificial Intelligence and Machine Learning in Marketing and Mobile Marketing.

Prior to joining Southampton University he was a Curriculum Area Manager and Business Development Director, Lecturer, entering Higher Education ten years ago. Before this time, he had a successful thirty-year commercial career as an international senior executive with Coca-Cola, Pepsi, Beecham, Timberland, Commonwealth Games, and Speedo International group of companies.

COPY RIGHT

Library of Congress – in – Publication Data

James Seligman, Southampton University,

Hampshire, England.

Mobile Marketing. James Seligman (PhD). Includes in

text and bibliography, references

ISBN: BOOK

'TO THOSE COMMITTED TO THE MARKETING TASK'

BOOK OBJECTIVE

The book is divided into chapter sections that logically walk the reader through mobile marketing. The book tries to give the reader the theory and practice behind the mobile marketing phenomena and provides supportive evidence of its growing importance.

From its history, statistical evidence and current trends the book exposes the subject matter in a way that is easy to appreciate and understand.

The audience for this book is considered to be scholars, teachers and students of marketing as well as practitioner seeking information on mobile marketing. It is a supportive aid for this topic to widen knowledge and understanding.

WHAT IS MOBILE MARKETING -1

OBJECTIVES

Chapter Learning Outcomes

To understand the concept of Mobile marketing and its importance in a technological driven marketplace where mobile devices are used together the information, communicate and allow the purchase of goods and services.

Critical thinking
Having completed this topic, one will be able to:
• Appreciate and understand the theory and practice behind Mobile Marketing.
• Start to understand the core frameworks
• Appreciate the size and scope of this marketing application

Having completed this topic, one will be able to:
• Discuss and debate mobile marketing
• Considers strategic options at a basic level

Just thinking about the fact that eighty per cent of internet users have their very own cell phone tells one that there is a communication platform opportunity. Both marketers and purchasers begin their internet services on mobile. Digital entrepreneurs specifically are excited to run cellular campaigns, due to the fact they recognize that mobile users are influenced consumers. According to Salesforce (2018) "sixtyeight per cent of agencies have incorporated mobile advertising into their average advertising method."

The advance is to start reaching out to them, and solving their problems, the greater outcomes you may get for one's business. It is no secret that building a mobile hit on-line enterprise has its challenges.

One is knowing a way to engage with customers on specific structures and devices.

It is not simple to get results out of mobile, however a very good understanding of ways mobile advertising works will position one in general control of your advertising.

The world of cell telephones has modified inside the past many years after Motorola made records while the FCC authorised the 8000X in 1983. This changed into the arena's first business transportable cellular smartphone. Its value to clients was a whopping $3,995 at the time. (FOX News Network, 2013). The first cellular phone changed into just a tool for making wi-fi phone calls however these days there are numerous more opportunities to apply on smartphone, and the rate is considerably increasing.

Within the past few years the amount of mobile smartphone customers has dramatically improved and Ericsson AB (2014) predicts that by way of 2020, ninety per cent of the global population over 6 years could have a mobile telephone, and phone subscriptions are expected to pinnacle 6.1 billion. Indicating evaluation that currently, cell phones is the smart tool accompanying built on a cellular running machine, with extra advanced computing functionality and connectivity.

The innovation of the mobile marketplace is being driven via 4 key factors: richer content material, community right of entry to for communications and content, extended bandwidth to enable this access, and new technologies (Heisterberg and Verma, 2014). Additionally, the technology is pushed by use tendencies, current megatrends, that regulate our lives.

MMA -The Mobile Marketing Association- (2009) defines mobile advertising and marketing as follows "Mobile advertising is a set of practices that enables groups to speak and engage with their audience in an interactive and relevant way through and with any mobile device or community." These set of practices are a way to talk with the client building up a deep interaction with a usually excessive client orientation.

Mobile is either push as well as pull advertising techniques. In pull advertising the consumer is already aware of the brand or product. The marketer is getting the patron to return to company purchasing a product or service. For example, Customer Relationship Management (CRM) is a good instance of pull method which may be additionally referred to as inbound advertising. Push advertising and marketing instead is that the consumer is being targeted. The consumer may not be aware about the services or products until the information approximately it is pushed at them via the advertising channel.

(TMR Direct, 2013) for example direct promoting to customers face to face is a good instance because marketers take the product to the patron.

Marketers need to understand purchaser behaviours, it is a good way to recognize the purchaser and how the customer buying decision process is going (Fahy and Jobber, 2012). Mobile technologies allow virtual entrepreneurs to interact with customers at each stage of the purchase path (Gartner, Inc., 2014).

In addition, mobile marketing may be a part of the multi-channel advertising which includes using a spread of engagement factors to create a seamless buying enjoyment for clients.

Those engagement factors encompass brick-and-mortar shops, websites, kiosks, smartphones, virtual signage, name facilities and social media (Bagal, 2012). Using alternative words groups use two or greater advertising and marketing channels to attain or extra consumer segments.

According to Gartner Inc. (2014) multichannel advertising represents a coordinated application throughout digital and conventional media to collect and preserve clients, expand the logo, situate the marketplace and have interaction groups.

This includes non-stop updates of the products management, care of the channel customers' records base as well as the choice and layout of the complete advertising mix. As mentioned via Fahy and Jobber (2012) advertising blend is a designed device to assist advertising making plans and execution, consisting four Ps: product, price, place, promotion.

Apart from the customers' comfort in purchasing from domestic or administrative centre at their handy time, the digital channel gives many advantages such as big statistics seeking in much less time and less effort, personalization, trouble-solving information, and so on (Dhotre, 2010).

Reported by means of Heisterberg and Verma (2014) mobile trade is an essential hyperlink between channels, especially for customers 18 to 34 years old, due to the fact smartphones are able to conduct matters including completing in-store and online purchases, unique offers, and notifying the stores while the client enters a shop. This is referred to as a more seamless and personalized go-channel. Mobile commerce is part of e-commercial enterprise with e-trade.

Let us begin with a brief definition. What is Mobile Marketing?

Mobile advertising encompasses the one spot which joins advertisers to consumers thru mobile gadgets and networks. Mobile gadgets encompass phones, PDAs, media devices, portable gaming consoles, tablet computer systems—and, of course, those gadgets which function as all of the above.

Some cellular devices can also be open to a few advertising and marketing channels (as an example, a fundamental cellular cell phone can receive textual content messages); even as other devices assist many extra opportunities, which include cell Internet get admission to, video messaging, and the potential to actively provoke and have interaction with advertising (as an instance, by way of scanning a QR code).

Andreas Kaplan defines cellular advertising as:

"Any advertising and marketing pastime performed thru a ubiquitous network to which purchasers are constantly linked the use of a private mobile tool." Wikipedia defines it as "marketing on or with a cellular tool".

Margaret Rouse defines it as:

"As a promotional activity designed for shipping to cellular phones, smartphones, and different handheld gadgets, commonly as an aspect of a multi-channel marketing campaign."

The author outlines mobile marketing "as marketing to mobile users using mobile electronic devices." (Seligman,2018)

As mobile gadgets end up being increasingly common, more groups are undertaking mobile advertising. The Mobile Marketing Association, a worldwide exchange association that promotes cellular marketing, represents greater than seven-hundred contributors, which includes service companies, advertisers, and types from a spread of industries.

Some examples of organizations and industries lively in mobile advertising consist of:

- Short Message Service (SMS)

- Multimedia Message Service (MMS)

- Quick Response (QR) Codes

- Location-primarily based Services (LBS)

- Push notifications

- Mobile advergaming

- Google, Yahoo, and different internet-based agencies

- Technology agencies which include Microsoft and Apple—indeed, Apple's I Products have been at once responsible for plenty of nowadays cell computing environment

- News media companies, which includes, FOX, CBS, the New York Times, and the Washington Post

- Sports media groups, along with ESPN, SKY

- Retailers, such as Best Buy and Target (at Best Buy, you can walk down the aisles scanning QR codes to get right of entry to online facts as you save)

- Brands, together with Proctor & Gamble, Coca-Cola, Pepsi, Mars, Ford.

Mobile advertising is defined as "the use of the cellular medium as a way of advertising verbal exchange" (Karjaluoto, Leppäniemil, 2005) or "distribution of any sort of promotional or advertising messages to consumer through wi-fi networks".

More particularly, it is "the use of interactive wireless media to provide clients with time and location sensitive, personalized facts that promotes goods, offerings and thoughts, thereby producing cost for all stakeholders" (Leppäniemil, 2008).

Mobile devices include cellular telephones, smart telephones, and tablets (along with Apple's iPad and Samsung's Galaxy Tab).
There are many types of mobile advertising and marketing including Short Message Service (SMS), Multimedia Message Service (MMS), In-game Mobile Marketing, Mobile Web Marketing, and Location-based Services. Technologies enabling mobile advertising include 3G, EDGE, GPRS, Wi-Fi, SMS, GPS and USSD.

3G networks allow network operators (consisting of AIS, DTAC and TRUE in Thailand) to provide users an extensive variety of more advanced offerings even achieving more community potential. Enhanced Data fees for GSM Evolution or EDGE allows data to be delivered at rates up to 384K bps via broad band. Generic Packet Radio Service or GPRS is a packet oriented cellular facts provider at the 2G and 3G cellular communique systems.

Wireless technology or Wi-Fi is the present day trend protocol for networking and connecting to the Internet. Global Positioning System or GPS presents reliable vicinity and time information using international navigation satellite TV for PC devices. Unstructured Supplementary Service Data or USSD works on all present GSM telephones, providing consultation-based communique, enabling an expansion of packages. (Quirk, n.d.)

Consumers have increasingly used mobile gadgets for communique, entertainment, business and statistics purposes.

Mobile advertising has modified distinctly from the past few years ago due to the appearance of recent technology and improved net infrastructures permitting more complete communications. BlackBerry, iPhone and Android telephones have modified the faces of mobile marketing in types of messaging, conversation, multimedia, and online companies.

For instance, the software referred to as WhatsApp is a move-platform cellular messaging application, which lets in users to change messages. WhatsApp customers do not pay for SMS charges however may pay for GPRS/ EDGE fees depending on terms and conditions through provider companies as WhatsApp requires Wi-Fi, EDGE/GPRS or 3G net connection.

An enterprise with customers' telephone numbers on a cellular cell phone can broadcast text messages, picture, voice, video, emoticons, and send to clients to inform them of latest promotions or new releases. Modern cell devices also offer users tools for chatting and verbal exchange along with MSN, Facebook Chat, Skype, Viber (for iPhone) and Kik Messenger. This has truly modified consumer lifestyles from merely indoor to any locations in the global with noticeably low communication charges.

Mobile gadgets also are prepared with wealthy multimedia packages that users can pick out to download for leisure and facilitation including hello-def video players (which includes mVideoPlayer which can play unique movie files on a cellular device), online radio stations (which includes TuneIn Radio that gives gateways to global radio stations), e-book readers (together with Aldiko and Amazon Kindle that permit readers to revel in unfastened and paid e-books).

News readers (along with All In One News) offers information updates from exceptional newspapers or information channels like BBC News, New York Times, Reuters, Wall Street Journal), TV channels (which include YouTube), file viewer (including Think Free Office that permits customers to view and alter files at the cross).

Users can truly proportion the contents they favour on their social networking internet websites. Moreover, the public can use cell gadgets for price of services and products through web sites or barcode scanning.

Ways of doing advertising and marketing have additionally immensely changed from the past. Businesses consider the usage of cellular advertising to include cell advertising, video games, online shops, and vicinity-primarily based services. Billions of cellular advertisements are introduced thru SMS, free cell programs and cellular webs in all components of the world.

According to (www.Techcrunch.Com 2018), BIA/Kelsey, adviser to agencies inside the local media enterprise, reviews that U.S. Cellular advertising sales will develop from $491 million in 2009 to $5 billion plus in 2018.

There are many cell applications used to experiment QR code (a two-dimensional matrix barcode evolved by Denso Wave and readable by way of QR barcode readers and digital camera phones) including BeeTagg, ShopSavvy and Barcode Scanner. After the code is scanned a mobile device, phone variety, messages, or net web site cope with the cellular display. Generated QR codes have regarded on exceptional media inclusive of posters, print advertisements, billboards, and even product applications for those curious to scan thru their mobile devices.

The latest technology known as Augmented Reality (AR), has additionally been added to the market, and has created a brand new manner of advertising. AR (consistent with Wikipedia.Org) is a term for a stay direct or an indirect view of physical, real-world surroundings whose elements are augmented via laptop-generated sensory enter, including sound or portraits. Agraphical3Dobjectfloatsfromthereal-international environment whilst considered thru a mobile device.

Application referred to as Layar uses the phone's digital camera and GPS capabilities to acquire statistics about the surrounding location.
Layar then displays information about restaurants or different websites in the place, covering these facts on the smartphone's screen (Bonsor, 2010).

More and greater people are getting mobile ads with the devices they convey and this form of enterprise nevertheless has a protracted ways to move.

Target advertising refers to the selection of unique segments to serve, and is a key detail in advertising approach according to Fahy and Jobber. (2012) Targeting cell defines solutions the way to target the target market thru the superior clever tools.

According to Krum (2010) focus on mobile refers to both figuring out key demographics and psychographics of marketer's supposed audience and adapting advertising messages to meet their desires. The intention of focus on cellular advertising is to create a proper marketing stimulus relating to the customers' on-line conduct. Thereby a maximum relevance of promotional messages may be provided.

Marketers distinguish their customers to know section groups based totally on customers' similarities. According to Abduljalil and Huam (2011) there are three ways to phase the target companies: —Those segmentations are ahead, backward and simultaneous. Forward segmentation starts with relating to similarities of intake services or products, backward segmentation starts off evolved with the aid of considering of similarities of purchasers' traits, and simultaneous is based totally on data among consumers' traits and scenario unique consumption patterns.

It is vital in mobile, that categories of purchasers' development are focused when they are widespread and need to be specific. The general characteristics are demographic, way of life and character, whereas precise characteristics shape with their attitudes, reviews, perceptions and preferences (Abduljalil and Huam, 2011). After this, goals of the organization became decided and analysed. An optimized suitable advertising and marketing campaign can then be implemented. Usually, the online focus is on frequently based on the use of cookies to gain records about the customers.

Summing up it is undisputed that targeting is vital for on-line agencies. According to Renner (2013) political barriers may additionally change the concentrated reason, —yet the provisions of the proposed EU safety law is not always fixed and could be better.

Four Customer Buying Decision Process

- Need Recognition/ Problem Awareness

- Information Search

- Evaluation of Alternatives

- Purchase

- Post- Purchase evaluation of selection

The five-step shopping for technique version from Fahy and Jobber (2012) suggests the buying process of customers. It is relatively vital for the marketers to recognize how their customers' behave so one can make them buy their merchandise. Smartphones have made the process tougher for entrepreneurs due to the fact people are constantly on-line.

In the first stage marketers have to make clients privy to messages for instance it might be banner advert in Google AdWords. According to Fahy and Jobber (2012) a marketer wishes to be privy to the wishes of customers and the needs they face as nicely inhibitors which impact human beings to transport on for the subsequent step of the shopping method.

For instance, marketers can affect client's emotions with promise to shed pounds however the fee can prevent purchaser to transport onto next step of the buying method. With cell advertising entrepreneurs can target the commercials extra efficiently.

Marketing online has modified the patterns of searching records and evaluating the alternatives.

According to Ferrell and Hartline (2014) the amount of time, effort, and cost dedicated to the search for facts relies upon the measure of danger concerned in the acquisition, the quantity of enjoyment the client has with the product, and actual fee of the hunt in time and money.

Potential customers can search for the goods even within the competitor's store to weight alternatives. Stated via Ferrell and Hartline (2014) customers examine merchandise as 'bundles of attributes' which have varying abilities to satisfy their wishes.

In cell advertising and marketing, customers can be everywhere, this makes it tricky to marketers. Smartphones have given massive benefit for customers to search information and examine the information due to the regular entry to the internet. For this reason agencies should take into account to use some of later described mobile marketing equipment, that they are visible everywhere and every time.

In the fourth step of the model, clients make a purchase and it may be everywhere and anytime via the opportunities of mobile marketing. Studies compare the consequences of what number of humans used the technique in a opposite form, that they first searched product on-line but in the long run purchased inside the physical store, this method is referred to as net-rooming. As seen within the both styles, customers had been making purchases using each method, and in recent research around 70 per cent of 19,000 respondents replied, yes.

Mobile phones are changing the manner your target audience and customers engage together with your brand. People visit your internet site on their telephones, open ones emails on smartphones, and buy out of the shop through their phones. Putting your commercial enterprise right in where your clients are – on the go – is what mobile advertising is all about. Any advertising plan these days that ignores mobile advertising is basically a failed plan.

REVISION

- In 100 words provide an overview on what is Mobile marketing.

- On a piece of paper describe the top ten items which make up Mobile marketing

- In 50 words explain how mobile marketing can be used. Use bullet points

A BRIEF HISTORY - 2

OBJECTIVES

Chapter Learning Outcomes
- To comprehend the history of mobile marketing (MM)
- To understand mobile applications in marketing today
- An appreciation of MM future in a marketing context

Critical thinking
Having completed this topic, one will be able to:
- Appreciate the development of MM and discuss it
- Have an appreciation of MM in marketing to date
- Be able to consider the future of MM

Critical thinking
Having completed this topic, one will be able to:
- Discuss and debate MM as a topic
- Analyse MM material and understand it
- Consider MM application in a work setting

Change is persistent in generations and groups who want to follow the developments to allow commercial enterprise fairness. Innovation is the manner of translating an idea or invention into a service or product that means the concept itself is not always innovation. Megatrends such as connectivity, ageing society, urbanization, globalization, new learning, individuality, fitness, sustainability and mega cities influence.

These megatrends already exist and will affect our lives for decades and will also dominating the mobile arena. The biggest developments effecting mobile advertising is connectivity which incorporates in addition defined Internet of Things (IoT) and Big Data.

Mass media channel: Smartphone
The mobile tool stands to be latest and greatest evolution of the media revolution (taken into consideration the seventh mass media) it imbibes the quality from all three monitors (cinema, TV, and the PC) and integrates and converges all six historic mass media: printing (1500s), recording (1900s), cinema (1910s), radio (Twenties), TV (Nineteen Fifties), and the net (Nineteen Nineties).

Gambhir (2013) cites the first cell phone was the Nokia Communicator, (Ahonen, 2013) cites that it turned into commonly focused for business use. Over the decade later, in 2007 the iPhone substantially changed the industry. The cell device itself has converted from a trifling communication device (or handset) to way of life phenomenon with convergence and divergence to a point as mentioned through Gambhir (2013).

Ericsson AB (2014) predicted that with the aid of the variety of telephone subscriptions will exceed those for primary phones, and it has.
Mobile is a distinct mass medium and gives lots of possibilities that the legacy of the net cannot supply (Ahonen, 2013).

According to Gambhir (2013) convergence across displays – usually TV, PC, and cell tool – it is essential to provide seamless entry. This has triggered that original consumer electronics (CE) devices to be changed to clever gadgets as an alternative because they are related to internet.

Main drivers of clever phones are discussed in following sections thinking about Big Data and Internet of Things. Mobile has become the quickest growth enterprise ever, to move from zero to $1 trillion in annual revenues (Ahonen, 2013). As made by means of (Zukunfts Intstitut, 2012) supports that in 2018 there had been 6 billion cell phone describers and the equal studies predicts that in 2020 there would be 8.1 billion smartphones.

One big motive for the massive increase is that there can be inexpensive smartphones and the rising of new markets in addition.

Technology Hype Cycle
Gartner's Technology Hype Cycle suggests some of the fundamental milestones of technology adaption. Gartner (2014) has analysed and forecast for exceptional types of technologies within the frames of time and expectancies.

The generation hype cycle has five most important stages and the first one is 'era trigger' which are primarily product prototypes. The next one 'the height of inflated expectancies' are actual products noticed by way of early adopters. In the third level, 'trough of disillusionment,' a proof of concept is missing and inflicting a downward slope.

'Slope of enlightenment technology' will become more widely understood and within the degree plateau of productivity the generation turns into broadly applied for every person.

Figure 1. Mobile Marketing Trends

Mobile Marketing Trends

Artificial Intelligence & Machine Learning
Learning, Automation, Cognition, Drones, Voice, Robots, SMART

Intense Deep Customer Experiences
Augmentation, Connected Places, VR, Holograms, 4D Print

Collection of Technology Choice
Block-chain, Big Data, 5G, TWIN, Neuro Transfer, Edge Computing

Implanted Devices
Wireless, Stimulators, Lenses, Trackers, Response

3. Big Data

Big Data refers to the masses of data gathered from interactions across the internet and devices. It is proven that it is presently in the starting off trough of 'disillusionment- degree' in which includes searching for proof of the concept, and it is predicted to extensively unfold in five to 10 years.

Big Data is defined by using its size, comprising a massive, complicated and independent collection of information units, each with the capability to interact. In addition, a crucial thing of Big Data is the fact that it cannot be handled with standard statistics management techniques due to the inconsistency and unpredictability of the viable mixtures (Apostu, 2012).

Big Data offers good sized feeds to organizations inclined to undertake it, but at the same time poses a significant range of challenges for the conclusion of such to gain value.

According to Assuncao (2014) corporations willing to apply analytics generation regularly collect high-priced software program licenses; employ large computing infrastructure; and pays for consulting hours of analysts who work with the corporation to better recognize its business, arrange its records, and integrate it for analytics.

This joint attempt of enterprise and analysts' regular pursuits to help the organisation understand its customers' desires, behaviours, and destiny demands for brand spanking new merchandise or marketing techniques. Stated by Eslinger (2014) the key to Big Data is to create small, intimate moments that build noticeably focused relationships with clients on an individual level.

Internet of Things
Internet of things is currently in its height of 'inflated expectancies' in which early adopters have diagnosed the real merchandise. It is expected that it will take as a minimum 5 years then it is going to plateau whilst the trend is broadly unfolded. This trend is all about making human lives easier.

Heisterberg and Verma (2014) define that Internet of Things (IoT) refers to uniquely identifiable objects and their virtual representations in an Internet-like shape. In alternative words: bringing the digital technology into life. For instance, robots with embedded sensors belong to earlier cited Mega Trend which impact the mobile advertising area.

As described, the Internet of Things maintains to confirm its essential position in the context of facts and conversation technologies and the development of society. Whereas standards and fundamental foundations had been elaborated and reached maturity, further efforts are necessary for unleashing the overall ability and federating systems and actors (Friess and Vermasan, 2013)

Figure 2.

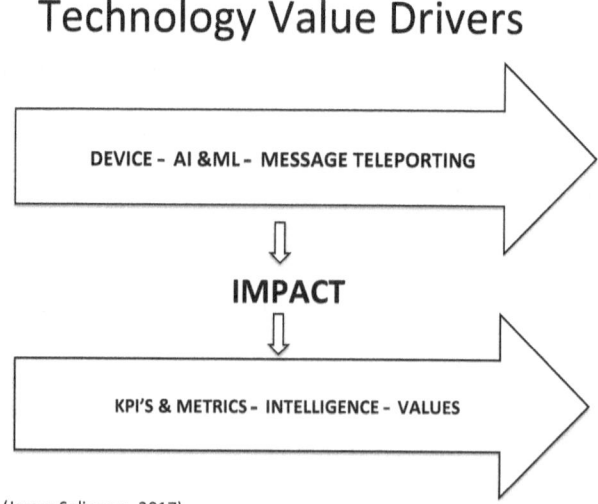

Technology Value Drivers

DEVICE - AI &ML - MESSAGE TELEPORTING

IMPACT

KPI'S & METRICS - INTELLIGENCE - VALUES

Copyright: (James Seligman, 2017)

There are a wide range of devices that can be used by organizations and consumers, it is a choice made to gain connectivity and reap embodied intelligence available. The data is accessed using artificial intelligence and machine learning using sensors and tags which use algorithms to identify, control, deliver. The device chosen by the sender or receiver focuses on access either via a network (s), cloud this is the message / data teleport. The value derived is the impact made from the process tools used which measures performance against logical KPI targets.

This leads to measurement of device use effectiveness and potential strategic re - alignment through knowledge gained.

The values gained differ from the sender and receiver, the sender measures value against the objectives set and devices used, the receiver measures value from the experience and benefits gained.

Most users take into account their cell phone almost as an intimate accent and preserve a very non-public dating with it (Bauer, Reichardt, Barnes & Neumann, 2005).

Teenagers explicit themselves in the society by their private fashion concerning clothes, music cultural fashion etc. (Willis, 2009) and their mobile telephone is not an exception.

These are personalized by deciding on a brand, length, colour, heritage image and ring tone that correspond to the owner's character. Mobile users hold their smartphone in reach 24 hours of the day, and it is considered a vital a part of their everyday lives (Bauer et al. 2005). Ahonen refers to a survey performed by means of BBDO in 2005 that revealed that 60% of all mobile telephone proprietors "go to bed with it". This is because of its utilization as an alarm clock, overdue night textual content messaging and night-time cell phone calls.

Another key fact of how vital the cellular cell phone is in our lives is revealed via by means of Unisys (Ahonen, 2008) that if we lose our wallet the average time reporting is 26 hours, however when losing our mobile phone we file in 68 minutes.

Due to the exact identification of the mobile telephone and its person made feasible via the SIM (Subscriber Identity Module) card, Bauer et al. (2005) consider that mobile telephones look like "the suitable medium for direct and personalized customer verbal exchange" in which the advertiser can attain the purchaser at any time and any region.

Mobile Generations
In pace with the developing era, cell phones and their use as a communication tool may be divided into four . Huang and Symonds (2009) describe these as "the 4 generations of cell advertising and marketing":

Mobile Voice (1st Mobile Generation)

In the early Nineteen Eighties the first era of mobile smartphone systems become launched, developed from the ideas of two-methods radios and now making mobile telephony available to the public (wikipedia. Com, 2018).

At the beginning of this generation the use of cell era to perform telemarketing associated sports became related to huge fees, but as time went by means of these fees were significantly reduced, encouraging brand proprietors in the use of the mobile platform. Compared to conventional fixed-line telemarketing it has also the additional benefits of personalization and mobility, making it feasible to reach the consumer at any location and any time (Huang & Symonds, 2009).

Mobile Messages (2d Mobile Generation)
The 2nd technology cell smartphone system commenced to emerge inside the Nineties, and differed from the first generation through the use of virtual transmission in preference to analogue. With this a brand new manner of verbal exchange turned into particularly textual content messaging or Short Message Service (SMS). This new approach of communicating became famous among the young and shortly spread across all ages. From an advertising manager's view, a brand-new verbal exchange device had emerged. This carrier made it possible to send textual content messages as a complement to voice communication, lowering the danger of wrong facts which can arise via the same.

Mobile Marketing – Smartphone as an advertising tool can build brand equity numerous substantial advantages in comparison to communication via voice which includes lower charges. Since the message is saved within the telephones it also has an extensively longer lifetime. It also makes it easier to talk crucial facts along with names, addresses and voucher numbers that may be difficult to recollect and without problems spelt incorrect. Finally the process of sending and receiving the messages may be made routinely.

Mobile Internet/Web (3rd Mobile generation)
The use of mobile phones was developing at a high pace and have become vast, it additionally became a massive part of consumer life, the use of it on a daily basis. The call for offerings grew and there has been an ever-growing demand for better statistics speeds. At the beginning of the 2000s this brought about increasingly more advanced cell phones admission to and excessive speed mobile broadband.

The new technology made way for cellular Internet advertising because of the possibility to surf the internet with the cell phone, beginning new, but unexplored, ways of the use of the cellular smartphone as a communique device. However, because of display size obstacles all internet sources cannot be displayed on mobile gadgets, making it necessary to evolve the assets to the device. (Huang & Symonds 2009)

Mobile Television (4th Mobile Generation)
In 2009, the call was for of high pace cell Internet, because of more and more bandwidth- extensive programs, it had grown to some extent where it have

become clear that a third cell period could not meet the call for it. The enterprise started to expand the fourth generation, with up to ten times the velocity capability of its predecessor and now in 2011 it is approximately to be introduced.

Even though cellular television has been around for multiple year, it is the main communication tool of the fourth technology. This technology has now not yet reached its complete ability due to the limitations of the 1/3 generation's network infrastructure. With accelerated capability in pace, cell tv advertising lets in "hi-tech involvement in the advertising tactics and, similarly, it hits the consumers' mental perception. The dynamic function of this type of verbal exchange channel lets in the dealers to replace the contents of their messages in real time; consequently, the contents are greater legitimate and accurate." (Huang & Symonds, 2009)

The cellular telephone as the seventh mass media
Ahonen (2008) describes the mobile smartphone as the 7th mass media channel. From simply being taken into consideration by using the hundreds as a voice device until the Nineteen Nineties, it emerged as a mass media channel. While being the youngest of the seven mass media it is also the least understood.

It is straightforward to underestimate the cell telephones as a mass media because of its tiny display and minimalistic keyboard, despite the fact that the mobile cell phone will prove the doubters incorrect as it is to the Internet what TV become to radio, "a far greater compelling and complete media platform that quickly will dominate".

The cellular smartphone is what Ahonen calls an "inherent danger" which has the that means of being "a media channel which could correctly offer all of the principle content types of all the preceding mass media". With the advanced cell telephones of today you can study newspapers, magazines and books, listen to radio, buy track and video games, watch TV or even complete length movies, regardless of where you are or what hour of the day.

4. SMS advertising

Marketing through mobile phones' SMS (Short Message Service) have become an increasingly popular within the early 2000s in Europe and a few components of Asia whilst organizations began to collect cellular phone numbers and send off wanted (or unwanted) content. On average, SMS messages are examined inside four minutes, making them rather convertible. The IAB (Interactive Advertising Bureau) and the Mobile Marketing Association, as well, have installed recommendations and are evangelizing using the cellular channel for marketers.

While this has been fruitful in evolved regions such as North America, Western Europe and a few different countries, cell SPAM messages (SMS sent to cellular subscribers without a valid and explicit decide-in by using the subscriber) remain an problem in many different parts or the sector, partly due to the carriers promoting their member databases to third parties.

SMS advertising services normally run off a quick code, however sending textual content messages to an e mail copes with any other methodology (even though this technique is not supported via the providers).

Short codes are five or 6 digit numbers, that have been assigned with the aid of all of the mobile operators in a given United States of America for the usage of emblem campaign and different purchaser offerings. Due to the high fee of quick codes of $500–$1000 a month, many small groups prefer to share a quick code on the way to reduce monthly expenses.

MMS
MMS cellular advertising can comprise a timed slideshow of photographs, textual content, audio and video. This mobile content is added through MMS (Multimedia Message Service).
Nearly all new telephones produced with a colour display can send and receiving fashionable MMS message.

Brands are able to each send (cell terminated) and receive (cellular originated) wealthy content via MMS A2P (application-to-man or woman) cellular networks to cellular subscribers. In a few networks, brands are also capable of sponsor messages which are despatched P2P (person-to-individual).

Push Notification
Push Notifications had been first added to smartphones through Apple with the advent of the I phone in 2007. They were later similarly popularized with the Android operational device, wherein the notifications are shown at the top of the display.

If not used wisely it is able to speedy alienate customers because it causes interruptions to their cutting-edge activities at the telephone in-recreation mobile advertising and marketing.
There are essentially 4 fundamental traits in cell gaming now: interactive actual-time 3-d video games huge multi-player video games and social networking video games.
This approach is a fashion towards more complicated and more sophisticated, richer recreation play which started out within the 1980's.

Mobile Web advertising

The Mobile Marketing Association provides a set of hints and requirements that give the endorsed layout of ads, presentation, and metrics used in reporting.

Google, Yahoo, and different foremost mobile content material vendors have been selling advertising and marketing placement on their devices for years.

QR codes

QR (or Quick Response) codes allow a customer to visit a web page and cope with it through scanning a 2D picture with their telephone's digicam, instead of manually getting into a URL. The resultant URLs normally include monitoring capabilities which would be unwieldy if typed through the purchaser. Originally accredited as an ISS standard in 1997, Denso-Wave first evolved the standard for tracking vehicle components in Japan.

Bluetooth

The upward push of Bluetooth started out round 2003 and a few companies in Europe have started out using it. Most of these companies offer "hotspot" structures which consist of a few type of content material-management device with a Bluetooth distribution function. This generation has the benefits that it is permission-based, has higher transfer speeds and is also a radio-based total generation and might consequently not be billed (i.e. Is freed from fee).

Infrared

Infrared is the oldest and most restricted form of mobile advertising. Some European agencies have experimented with "purchasing window advertising and marketing" through loose Infrared waves within the 90s. However, infrared has a very limited variety (~ approx. 10 cm – 1meter) and will in no way at present actually set up itself as a leading Mobile Marketing generation.

Location-based totally services

Location-primarily based offerings (LBS) are presented by a few cellular telephone networks as a way to send custom marketing and other data to mobile-phone subscribers based totally on their contemporary vicinity.

The cell-phone carrier provider gets the region from a GPS chip built into the smartphone, or the use of radio location and tri lateration based on the signal-electricity of the nearest cellular-smartphone towers (for phones without GPS features).

In the United Kingdom, which launched region-primarily based offerings in 2003, networks do now not use trilateration.
 LBS services use a single base station, with a 'radius' of inaccuracy, to decide a cell phone's place.

User Controlled media

Mobile advertising differs from most other varieties of advertising and marketing communique in that there are frequent user (patron) initiated (cell originated, or MO) messages, and calls for the express consent of the client to obtain destiny communications, it commenced round 2007.

A call delivered from a server (commercial enterprise) to a person (client) is called a cellular terminated (MT) message. This infrastructure factors to a trend set by way of cellular marketing of purchaser managed advertising and marketing communications.

The history of cellular marketing links back to the time when the primary commercial mobile SMS and short codes had been released in 2003.

Pontiac and Nike were the primary two brands that released SMS campaigns in 2005. This became the time when each manufacturer realized that mobile marketing is the destiny, due to the fact consumers have been using cellular phones to communicate, find, buy goods and services.

By 2007, there have been 2.4 billion SMS customers in use around the globe. Apple launched its first iPhone inside the US and QR codes had been incorporated into mobile advertising in 2010, which brought about the beginning of a new dynamic generation in advertising.

By 2011, cellular advertising becomes a $14 billion dollar international enterprise.

By 2013, Android and iOS had dominated the marketplace and it is the time when apps have been become famous and smartphones had been replacing conventional mobile phones.

By 2014, the range of mobile cell phone customers passed the variety of laptop users and those who were gaining access to the net from their telephones.

Today, some eighty-nine per cent of cell time is spent on apps while the closing eleven per cent is spent on web sites. This is the primary motive why seventy-one per cent of recently surveyed marketers say that mobile advertising is core to their enterprise, at the same time as sixty eight per cent brands have included cellular advertising and marketing into their standard advertising and marketing method.

Brands that lack a mobile advertising strategy must reconsider their marketing method, due to the fact all such brands are dropping customers each second of the day.

REVISION

- Using 100 words describe how Mobile marketing has developed and grown

- Provide a definition of QR codes.

OBJECTIVES

With the growth of mobile devices and the change in consumer lifestyles people are more mobile and more difficult to reach than traditional media. Mobile marketing provides a solution to marketers by utilising Communication forms on Mobile devices.

Chapter Learning Outcomes
* To comprehend why MM is vital
* To understand MM importance in marketing today
* An appreciation of MM benefits in a marketing context

Critical thinking
Having completed this topic, one will be able to:
* Appreciate the importance of MM and discuss it
* Have an appreciation of MM in marketing to date
* Be able to consider MM as a process
* Discuss and debate MM as a topic
* Analyse MM metrics and understand it
* Consider MM application in a work setting

Why is mobile marketing so essential today? One may not be completely be aware of the facts, however let us review some of the motives to pay undivided attention to this phenomena?

"In 2018 mobile internet traffic was fifty-one per cent of total global online, with social media total mobile minutes at twenty-one per cent in the USA coming off 2017. Mobile internet penetration rate in 2017 was over sixty-five per cent in selected key countries with eighty per cent in the UK and seventy-five per cent in the USA.

Global mobile data traffic has grown from seven per cent to seventeen per cent in 2018 and forecasted to hit forty-nine per cent by 2021" (statistica, com,2018).

The mobile app market is also growing with shopping leading, followed by music and entertainment with overall average growth of six per cent. Looking at tablets and smart phones, smart phones are at least twice as large in activity use clearly led by e-mail on smart phones at fifty-nine per cent of users.
Trust is a key component of mobile apps over thirty-seven per cent of users have a choice with forty two per cent they trusted apps because data could be

deleted. Global mobile media traffic is expected to grow from 7.2 to 38.1 terabytes per month, significant growth.

In January 2018 in the UK, mobile social media penetration was fifty-seven per cent, by 2019 some twelve billion pounds will be spent on mobile e-commerce. Europe trails Asia (No1) and North America (No2) in social network penetration showing this area is ripe for growth with the global average growth in 2018 at thirty-nine per cent.

This is convincing evidence mobile marketing by smart phone or mobile PC is a huge marketplace full of consumers, however, there is more:

1) Reach: When reach is a difficult, there's nothing easier than a cellular phone to attain your target audience. In a recent US survey seventy-nine per cent phone users stated that their telephone is the primary element they take a look at in the morning, next is going to the bathroom at twenty seven per cent, and that they preserve their smartphone near them in the course of the day. But that is now not all.

An average US cellular telephone consumer spends ninety minutes an afternoon on their smartphone, whilst America customers spend a great deal of time 'up to 220 minutes' a day on their phones whilst time in browsers decreased by fifty per cent. Most interesting is that ninety per cent of all incoming SME's are read within three minutes.

This average time is increasing each day since 2014, (flurry analytics, 2015). This trend is consistent in most major countries. There could not be a less complicated manner to attain your customers. You can reach them anywhere, repeatedly, as long as you have got a solid mobile advertising strategy in process. Mobile marketing 'reaches' in which other advertising and marketing channels certainly do not.

2) Personal: A mobile smartphone is a personal tool. According to a research study, ninety one per cent of mobile cell phone users maintain their cell phone within one arm's reach for the duration of the day. (Connor, 2013, Nov,12 Forbes.com). When you connect with your purchasers through mobile, your brand is put inside the same class as the 'pals and circle of relatives of that person.' People join better with brands that set up a one-on-one connection with them, and there is not anything higher than a cell smartphone to build this very private connection.

3) Instant: If you need to ship a message immediately for your clients, what medium might you pick out?

Research shows that ninety per cent of the textual content messages are in review in much less than 3 minutes, even as others take a look at, it become shown that textual content messages have ninety eight per cent open rate.

Mobile marketing does not simply have super attainment it offers the message immediately. Unlike e mail advertising in which reaction is just six per cent, textual content messages have a notable response rate of forty-five per cent. Text messages are added instantly, are read instantly, and produces astonishing consequences for brands.

4) Mobile ecommerce: Consumers pick shopping from their cellular devices. More than forty-four per cent of time spent more than the net on cellular telephones. As high as seventy-eight per cent of cell phone searches resulted in a purchase. This compares with sixty-one per cent on PC and laptop.

"Mobile commerce is swiftly developing as a dynamic marketing communications channel and is expected to dominate e-commerce in the future" (Seligman, 2017).

Mobile commerce attributes thirty-four per cent of world e-commerce in 2016, and it's predicted to grow thirty-one per cent with the aid of new processes in 2017/18.

There is no excuse for corporations to nevertheless forget about cellular marketing. Here some sound logical reasons:

5) Cost-effective: Mobile marketing is extraordinarily price effective as compared to other advertising and marketing techniques.
For example, placing an ad on TV is highly priced form of communication than strolling a SMS marketing campaign or growing a mobile optimized internet site. So one should make extra cash in the long run.

6) Customer engagement: The customers will agree mobile offers a better amazing experience along with your brand on their cell telephones. Research indicates that sixty-one per cent of people expand a pleasing opinion of manufacturers after they do now not face any problem touring the website from their mobile phones. While thirty per cent of customers will depart your website if it is not optimized for cellular.

Nowadays, globalization has made it harder for companies to survive at the side of the excessive velocity of technological development, which has extended the pace of product imitations (Melin & Hamrefors, 2007). This phenomenon has increased by way of the evolution of the Internet and mobile which has appreciably altered advertising practices (Winer, 2009).

Thus, experiencing a shortened product lifestyles-cycle, business groups need to find a further factor that attracts customers, apart from product superiority itself (Melin & Hamrefors, 2007).

In this quest of gaining aggressive brand benefits, a business enterprise has a confined range of alternatives that provide it with long-time period of dominance. Among those, an advantage with an extremely longer time- span is constituted by way of 'purchaser orientation' and a 'robust emblem or name' (Kapferer, 2008).

The concept of patron orientation results in the connection of advertising and marketing paradigm, which is seen as an essential detail that organisations need to use, to deal with the turbulences and complexity of the enterprise environment (Patterson & O'Malley, 2006).

As defined through Hougaard & Bjerre (2003), relationship marketing is "organisation behaviour with the motive of setting up, keeping and developing aggressive and profitable client relationships to the advantage of each". While it sets up obstacles via limiting the scope to employer conduct, thereby excluding as an example, broader standards just like the typology of relationships, it is sufficient to allow for discussion. Even if the concept itself can refer to the relationship of a corporation with six key markets, particularly, internal, customer, referral, dealer, influencer and employee recruitment markets (Veloutsou, 2002).

Within the connection advertising paradigm, it is underlined that customers build relationships with brands, not with agencies. Thus, one can understand the importance of manufacturers of brands, their definition should be clear. The American Marketing Association (AMA) defines a brand / emblem as —a call, time period, layout, image, or some other feature that identifies one seller or provider from those of different sellers (AMA, 2012). But this does not give sufficient justice to the complexity of brands.

This complexity is expressed through Achenbaum (1993) who adds that "what distinguishes an emblem from its unbranded commodity counterpart and offers is fairness, it is the sum of purchasers " perceptions and emotions about the products attributes and how they perform, about the emblem sense and what it stands for, and about the business enterprise associated with the logo." In the identical mind-set, Kapferer (2008) stresses the brand's emotional factor, that is based totally on a mind-set of non-indifference in the customers' hearts. Hence, the emblem will become a promise that the business enterprise is committing to constantly and that have to be continually sustained to keep customers glad (Rowley, 2004b).

Based on these views and given the focal point of this section at the brand-emblem relations, a logo is called: a differentiating sign or symbol, containing a total of customers perceptions and emotions that generate a mind-set.

Thus, the brand purpose is to underline the relational aspects of a brand - emblem interaction, which are inspired by means of all of the logo's values that shape clients perceptions.

Given the above-offered attributes, the overall aim of building a strong brand / emblem is to create meaningful relationships and thereby have a wide basis of unswerving clients through underlining the added value and the capability to meet customer wishes (Melin & Hamrefors, 2007).

This is in accordance with the mentality that —purchaser fairness is the preamble of financial fairness (Kapferer, 2008) based on the fact that the more people recognize and believe the emblem / brand, the more its impact upon the market.

Hence, the consumer-brand courting is visible as a prerequisite for emblem survival, revolving around purchaser self-belief (Harun et al., 2010) and logo loyalty (Brown, 2000).

As Morgan and Hunt (1994) provide an explanation for customer trust and commitment together decorate productiveness, efficiency and effectiveness, as this mixture of cooperation from the companions of the relationship is ensured. Moreover, a sturdy customer-brand will allow the logo to set a price premium due to the added value perceived via customers (Campbell, 2008).

Consequently, this leads to a monetary rise and also ensures a top market function for the organization. This implies, a protracted-time period approach that considers loyalty and repeat commercial enterprise as the basis of sustainable growth (Kaplan, 2011).

From the consumer's attitude, the advantage is in the added value. As Phipps (2011) indicates, the emblem is a super-product, imagined to upload value to the patron with the aid of selling interactivity via the manner of a tighter collaboration among the consumer and the logo, this is where mobile works really well.

Furthermore, Kapferer (2008) reinforces this concept by mentioning that a logo name and its image contains all the meanings created through customers' stories, its merchandise, its shops, its communications and personnel. Therefore, it can be concluded that branding has a relationship constructing position, leading to a win-win situation for each the corporation and the purchaser using mobile marketing.

Given the complexity of the enterprise surroundings these days, many entrepreneurs and researchers have been looking for a solution using mobile advertising through making use of this approach (Ortiz & Harrison, 2011). For example, Fournier (1998) analyses the client- brand relation inside the same manner as relationships among human beings.

In her studies, Fournier for that reason categorizes relationships as an example arranged marriage, regarding lengthy-time period, loyal relationships. This seems an intuitive method, thinking about the human nature of researchers; consequently, this perspective is being taken into consideration and is very beneficial, as it is supposed to result in an in-depth information of ways the consumer- brand relationships are constructed (Patterson & O'Malley, 2006). In this mind-set, the connection is described with the aid of Fournier (1998) as a reciprocal trade related to mutual benefits.

Moreover, it is considered as purposive and offering meaning to its active and interdependent parties. Subsequently, it is seen as a procedure, which evolves and undergoes modifications in line with the interactions that take vicinity among the partners. Thus, for Fournier, consumer-logo relationships and human relationships are synonymous.

However, on the practitioners' side, critiques seem to be divided as many marketers show scepticism in the direction of the declaration that customers and brands can create genuinely significant relationships. Baskin (2012) as an example criticizes this approach of evaluating brands to human beings.

They have a persona and customers cannot have a communication with it. Instead, they see manufacturers as the outcome of business enterprise actions and customers' perception of them.

From this point of view, there might be no client - brand relation. However, the life of a purchaser - brand courting is seen as a prerequisite; despite the fact that, the authors nevertheless maintains open thoughts, not qualifying every interplay between the consumer and the emblem as a relationship. Nowadays, this purchaser-brand relation has been increasingly more stimulated by using the Internet and mobile, and hence should be analysed in this context.

Even if Phipps (2011) and Kapferer (2008) do no longer specifically talk to this medium for the brand reports and interactivity, Winer (2009) underlines that the Web 2.0 and 3.0 is a propitious channel that enables their introduction. Thus, at the same time as interactivity, collaboration and brand stories represented a difficult challenge to perform via marketers through traditional media, they are now more effortlessly doable inside the Internet and mobile context.

However, to apprehend how the patron-brand courting is built online, one should first study how relationships were built in traditional offline advertising and marketing; especially which demanding situations had been related to these tools. This is critical which will appreciate the effect that the evolution of the Internet and mobile had on the customer-emblem relationship.

Mobile

Companies' interactions with customers are increasingly managed by technologies that enable the firms to personalize communications in real time across multiple media platforms and channels. Thus, marketing communications is nowadays increasingly interactive by nature (Bezjian-Avery et al. 1998). Interactive media changes marketing communications from a one-way process to a two-way process with the interaction of the consumer and marketer at the core (Stewart & Pavlou 2002).

This view of interactive marketing is obviously motivated by Integrated Marketing Communications (IMC), Kitchen et al. (2004). During the past decade, IMC has generated an increasing interest among academics and practitioners. From an interactive marketing viewpoint, IMC not only defines and assigns the integrated role of diverse communication media but also addresses how the combination of different media enhances the overall effectiveness of a firm's customer relationships.

Given this new communications environment, marketers are increasingly using new, interactive and highly targeted media (Barwise & Farley 2005). Besides the Internet, mobile media presents interesting opportunities for marketers by providing new possibilities for interacting with existing and potential customers.

Indeed, mobile marketing, where mobile (wireless) media is used as a content delivery and direct response channel in integrated campaigns along with traditional media such as a TV, radio, and print, or as a standalone medium. The new paradigm is increasingly interactive by nature (Peltier et al. 2003).

In fact, the dramatic rise of new electronic media has drastically altered marketing communications planning in general and IMC specifically. Integrated Marketing Communications (IMC) is gaining increasing interest among academics and practitioners.

According to Kitchen et al. (2004), IMC has grown in recognition and importance for effective marketing. This is due, in large part, to the fact that marketers are increasingly allocating budgets away from mass media due to the increased media fragmentation (Kotler et al. 2005) and increasing segmentation of consumer needs and preferences (Durkin & Lawlor 2001).

Easier access to consumer databases and data mining developments (Kitchen & Shultz 1999), the significance of customer loyalty via relationship marketing (Schultz 2002) and the importance of building and increasing a brand's image-based equity, Schultz 1999).

Explanation of IMC falls in four core areas (Kliatchko 2005).

(1) IMC is both a concept and a process

(2) IMC requires the knowledge and skills of strategic thinking and business management

(3) IMC is hinged on and distinguished by three essential elements or pillars – audience-focused, channel-centered and result-driven

(4) IMC involves an expanded view of brand communications

These elements are in line with the five facets of IMC summarized by Shimp (2000):

(1) aims at affecting behavior

(2) starts with customers or prospects

(3) uses any and all forms of contacts

(4) achieves synergy

(5) builds relationships.

Marketers and communicators frequently use multiple communication tools and/or channels within a single campaign. This is due, in a large part, to the fact that using multiple communication tools can be mutually reinforcing, or "synergistic" (Naik & Raman 2003). Thus, the ultimate goal of employing multiple communication vehicles is to have them synergize in order to create the greatest persuasion effect (Caywood et al. 1991).

Nonetheless, achieving a positive return on a marketing communication investment is becoming harder as the dynamics of markets change. A number of issues that affect how customers respond to marketing offers and how marketing communication is managed have been identified (Duncan & Mulhern 2004).
These include (Reid 2005):

- reduced faith in mass marketing as marketing communication channels fragment and consumer brand and media loyalties diminish or dilute

- increasing reliance on more highly targeted marketing communication methods to reflect a growing "relationship-marketing" orientation in many organizations

- increased turnover of brand-management personnel and a subsequent loss of learning and knowledge regarding consistent promotional strategy and market experience

- greater demand placed on marketing communication agencies to become brand custodians or guardians rather than simply transaction-based suppliers of marketing communication services

- increased efforts to measure and improve marketing communications return on investment (ROI), reflecting greater demands by both agencies and clients for accountability and measurement of alternative customer acquisition and relationship activities.

In summary, the initial conceptualizations of IMC were somewhat blurred and led to the adoption of different approaches to creating messages (Carlson et al. 2003).

Mobile optimized internet site and better cell advertising approach will not simply grow income, but you will have a pool of happy clients who will keep on with your brand for years yet to come.

REVISION
- Using your own words, in 100 words explained the full benefits of

    Mobile marketing.

- In 50 words explain how mobile marketing can be cost-effective.

OBJECTIVES
Literature explains how mobile marketing operates, it's growing importance and the benefits that can be achieved using MM in a marketplace.

Chapter Learning Outcomes
- To comprehend the elements of MM
- To understand MM tools in marketing today
- An appreciation of MM in a marketing context

Critical thinking
Having completed this topic, one will be able to:
- Appreciate the development of MM and discuss it
- Have an appreciation of MM in marketing to date
- Be able to consider the future of MM in a business context

Critical thinking
Having completed this topic, one will be able to:
- Discuss and debate MM as a topic
- Analyse MM operation and understand it
- Consider MM application in a work setting

Data from the study of smart phones show that they are used to search by eighty per cent of respondents only eleven per cent use PC and laptops. This means most consumers are using mobiles to search for information including goods and services.

Mobile marketing takes advantage of multi channels as a strategy at reaching as many target consumers as possible on smart phones, tablets, and other mobile devices using we sites, e-mails, SMS, MMS, Apps, and social media. Mobile is a disrupter using a mobile screen.

Mobile has speedily emerged as key, and as such, enterprise proprietors and executives want to respond and adapt to this fact through streamlining advertising and marketing techniques to maximise their benefits and capitalise on possibilities for addition enterprise and financial increase.

You have interaction in cellular marketing while you design and impact promotional activities aimed at cell gadgets to meet your unique business and advertising and marketing goals, in addition to further your advertising campaigns across exceptional cell systems and/or channels.

Design and effect an effective mobile marketing approach by using:
- Mobile-friendly website(s)
- Mobile-friendly content

- Deals, treats, and coupons
- Mobile fee options
- Mobile-only social
- Maximise in your unique techniques
- Text/Short Message Service (SMS) advertising and marketing
- Mobile-friendly website online(s)

Marketers have now discovered that mobile is king.

So, first things first: make certain all your sites are mobile-prepared and cellular-responsive. Customers and your target marketplace now want to pinch, zoom, scratch, and tick off their purchases, even their gadgets wish list. This fact has prompted groups to make certain their websites are mobile consumer-pleasant and continue to be so.

But right here is the key element: your cell website should not be just be fun, it should also seriously bear in mind streamlining customers' checkout techniques and ensuring it's easier and faster to achieve this.

One does that by means of decreasing your bandwidth length—not considered one of your pages ought to be slow loading, as mobile users are less affected persons than those using desktops/PCs.

Logins using your clients' social media accounts assist and make the method faster and greener. You might also include an alternative where customers can login the usage of their Facebook, and when they are in the site, make certain they are hooked.

Remember, customers who are afforded the time to rethink and reprocess their purchases are more likely to re-shelve items or delay the complete purchasing process.

Also, developing your personal cell app will no doubt accentuate all the above strategies and more. Online publications are on hand to help you in designing and customising even only a primary app, for starters.

If not, you can lease a developer or pick a relied upon app development employer to design your personal cell app—these types of options are to be had to you whether you are on a completely confined price range or your corporation can spare a good sized budget.

Mobile-friendly content material
Produce content primarily based in your market and needs analyses. Ask yourself: what do my clients need and need to see whilst on the move? Unlearn computer writing—all your tabs, pages, hyperlinks, and different auxiliary website online components are now not compatible.
Despite this widespread use of mobile devices, some marketers have yet to optimize their websites, ads and images for mobile success. Here are three ways to ensure you are ready to face the mobile-heavy marketing world of

2018.

Here are some easy approaches to make sure your content material works for your mobile clients:

1. Do not Forget the Headlines
Boring headlines do not get you a long way with web users and they actually will not do a whole lot for mobile cell users. Remember, cell users are on-the-move, so that they are searching out something that catches their interest. That said, your headline desires to be catchy, compelling, and re-tweetable. It also wishes to be smooth to read on a small screen.

For excellent results, keep your headline informative and specific. It needs to inform the reader precisely what they will gain. Skip the lovable or mysterious headlines – your cellular readers do not have time to discern out what you're attempting to mention.

2. Hook Them with the Introduction
It tells the cell reader what the content material is about and allows them determine whether or not to paste round. As such, it ought to be informative and thought motivating for your reader and must reveal the reader wants.

3. Remember Not All Screens Are the Same
Mobile devices have small screens, create content material that makes your target market take notice. When it involves writing your cell material, you need to be direct, succinct, and to the point.

Readers do not need impenetrable walls of text or impossible-to-find menus. Everything has to be simple to locate, accessible for your customers, and smooth to navigate.

Pay unique interest to how your pictures and menus show up on cellular gadgets, as these are trouble areas that may make or wreck the mobile enjoy. For first-rate results, write your content material for the internet, and then preview it on a small display. Does it seem to be in the manner you wanted it? Are there any glitches or mistakes that hold one from searching? If so, repair it before the content goes stay.

4. Divide Your Content into Chunks
Everything you create for a cell platform should be easy to study. This approach needs the text will should be moved into small chunks so cellular users can skim it effortlessly.

Do not overlook to use bolded headlines, numbered or bulleted lists, and brief paragraphs to beautify clarity.

5. Test Your Content, Then Test It Again
The biggest mistake content material creators make with mobile fabric is failing to test it once it goes live. Even the greatest content material can be made better, and plenty of content material creators might find that even an

easy tweak to their headline or structure could make a large difference in clicks and leads.

Use A/B Testing Tools to check exceptional versions of ones on line content. Be certain that one is best converting or changing a single piece of your content, so that you can accurately tune what's making a distinction.

One will additionally need to pay cautious attention to live audience feedback. Do they like your cellular content or are they having issues with it? Address any pain points your readers may additionally have.

Responsive Design: A Must-Have, for Mobile Users
While making your content readable on a mobile devise is vital, you will additionally need to include responsive design to get the maximum ROI from your website.

Responsive design essentially indicates that your website online is conscious of cellular users on exclusive gadgets.
When your web site is incredibly responsive, you run a lower danger of losing customers for a loss of functionality, and a higher chance of turning more traffic into customers.

A website online that is built on a responsive device pays interest to such things as screen length and determination. It routinely adjusts primarily based at the desires of the person to offer them the greatest enjoyment. That approach text, media, and even videos shift automatically so that the whole thing operates flawlessly in your website.

Why Use Responsive Design?
Much like writing mobile cell-pleasant content is essential these days responsive layout is also key. Here is why:

It is Recommended by Google. While there's been a few hypotheses approximately whether it is a rating factor, Google has made it clear they choose responsive sites.

Responsive Sites Are Indexed Faster. Indexing can take place extra hastily when bots don't have multiple URLs to drawl through.

You will Save Time and Money on Website Development. Since responsive web sites self-adjust to numerous mobile structures, once settled one should spend as a great deal time altering your website online down the road.

It's Simple. Today, you may use one CMS to load the whole thing you want for your site and maintain it for this reason.

While building a responsive website online would possibly appear hard, it is an integrated capability with CMSs from WordPress to HubSpot, and it will be a hands-off process until you decide to construct your web page from the floor up.

The Future of Mobile-Friendly Material

There's no doubt about it: cellular is the marketing communications manner of the future.

If you are not writing content material for your cellular target audience, you are wasting advertising money on material that does not cater in your audience's desires or needs. What is more, for this reason cellular adoption have skyrocketed in current years, and display no sign of slowing down soon, investing in mobile content material is simply plain properly commercial enterprise, and it will gain you for years yet to come.

Right now, it's time to start questioning mobile. One's website and the enterprise depend on marketing functionality to attract the cell target market, and it's time to leap in. Fortunately, it is simpler than it might appear, and developing splendid cell content is easy. Bear in mind that mobile gadgets display content material on smaller, more restrained displays.

So, make certain your content is easy however engaging. An effective content material combines crisp and attractive visuals—photos or movies—with honest, relevant, and minimal textual content. Your goal is to engage your cutting-edge customers and your future ones, inspiring them to act upon seeing/experiencing your mobile content. The favoured action, of direction, is them purchasing/availing your products/offerings.

Deals, treats, and coupons

Never underestimate the strength of freebies and the traditional—but nonetheless very powerful—coupon. Now, moreover, one can utilise mobile coupons. Recent studies display around ninety-six per cent of mobile clients still use coupons, and cellular coupon redemption price is even ten instances higher than mag-clipped coupons.

Reach and engage your mobile target market via using cell coupons, treats, deals, and even freebies! When you incentivise your mobile customers, you're also ensuring you are increasing revenue by way of using SMS and e-mail push notifications.

Greater redemption is determined in promos sent whilst a goal patron is near a store's region or has simply long gone through your web site. Promotions are available in all shapes and sizes, but we've broken them down into 5 classes: discounts, spending, shopping for, free and different.

Here is a listing of the offer kinds that work best:

Discount Offers

1. Discount Percentage on Purchase Total: This is one of the best to distribute. Simply discount a per cent off the full purchase rate.

The offer might be 10% off, so it does now not matter if clients spend one hundred or five: it is an equal bargain. Example: Get 20% off your purchase.

2. Discount on precise object: Just like the preceding offer, except as opposed to the acquisition total, the bargain most effective applies to a particular object. Example: Get 20% off one item.Spending Offers

3. Spend X and get a per cent bargain on overall purchase: Very common in offers within the retail space. If you spend a certain sum of money, you will get a per cent off the whole buy. This is an offer which could assist bump up cart length drastically. Example: Spend one hundred and get 10% off your complete buy.

4. Spend X and get a set quantity of credit score: Spend X and get X is a first-rate manner to get clients to purchase any other object. Example: Spend a hundred and get $ / £20 of credit.

5. Spend X and get an object free: Great way to growth cart size via providing an object that a person would love but may not buy. Example:
Spend one hundred and get a free scarf

Buying Offers

6. Buy X, get X free: Any variant of Buy 1 get 1 Free plays well. For retail apparel, it frequently makes experience to provide Buy 1 of an item to get a 2d free since the consumer would possibly want the equal piece of apparel in special colours. Example: Buy one shirt get a second one free.

7. Buy X, get Y unfastened: Another variant of the BOGO this is usually suited extra in the direction of restaurants. Example: Buy one menu item and get a free order of fries.

8. Buy X get Y discounted: Not quite a BOGO however nonetheless extraordinary. This works properly whether or not the primary item is greater or less high priced than the second one. Great for retailers who want to doubtlessly promote gadgets that normally cross together. Example: Buy any 2018 coat and get 15% off boots.

Free Offers

9. Free Shipping: Free delivery is a sort of treat. The cost is regularly small but it removes a sizable headache. Example: Free Shipping if you order these today.

10. Free session: This is not unusual offer for service agencies. One can even have seen this used quite often within the research space wherein, if one buys a document, one is offered a consultation. This is a first-rate way to get in touch with clients. Example: Free session if you buy this file.

11. Rebate Coupon: Rebates are the favourite type because they require extra effort at the purchaser's part, but the margin is typically higher because now not one hundred per cent of people will mail in the rebate coupon. Example: lower price if one sends back with mail-in rebate.

12. Totally Free object: This is a very uncommon offer kind and is ordinarily used as a PR move, along with McDonalds presenting coffee inside the morning hours, or Ben & Jerry's presenting cost free ice cream. Example: Come on in this Tuesday for a free espresso.

Other Offers

13. Loyalty Special: Many of the items above may be utilized in a loyalty program, but do not forget to provide specific rewards for customers who can show some form of club or fame. Example: All VIP Club individuals get 20% off their buy this week. If you are no longer a member sign up right here.

14. Personal Information offer: Sharing records in return for a proposal is a first rate way to incentivize customers to proportion alternatives, place and greater. Example: Reply with your e mail to the deal to get a further $20.

15. Refer a chum: Granting customers credit score or extra services for all they refer, has been tremendously successful for brands like Dropbox and Uber. Whether it's greater storage space, money or entries into a sweepstakes, referring people is a sure-fire way to generate interest. Example: Refer a friend and five credit score for all of us who signs up.

16. Dynamic coupons: This is the cutting fringe of coupons: providing coupons whose fee may additionally shift. This consists of game coupons, consisting of scratchers or spin-to-win video games, as well as time-based totally coupons where the user has a clock countdown to use the coupon, with the provide changing every second. Example: scratch cards.

Nothing engages your customers higher than the words "free" and "extraordinary deal."

Whilst using some of these strategies, one can continue to hold a sharp sense of commercial enterprise. Only continue with freebies and treats one considers positive and will convey greater price and desire for your commercial enterprise.

Mobile payment alternatives
It is a given your customers could want the quickest, most handy, but nevertheless the most secure manner to transact. To make sure you cater to this demand, you want to make mobile price alternatives in your websites and pages. This is important in case you want your business to remain relevant and thriving.

Make positive all of your offerings receive and are without difficulty, handy with the aid of cell gadgets, even smart watches! Make sure, though, that your cellular price security is the strong.

Techradar.com,(2018) cite the idea of a 'digital wallet' which has been promised for years, sooner or later making the cell phone the most essential item to have when leaving the residence.

However, up till lately, just about all transactions were performed through greater traditional fee methods, namely credit and debit pay cards, in addition to vintage trusted hard currency.

Mobile charge apps are changing the old school manner of purchasing, and streamlining the system. They excel at small transactions, averting the want for having cash, such as paying a babysitter, or splitting the tab at a restaurant when dining with friends.

Mobile bills also are getting used at retail establishments, thru contactless price structures and Near Field Communication (NFC).

Here are highlighted the mobile card price readers of 2018

1. Apple Pay

iOS meets cashless. Apple loves to make the complicated simple and clean for anybody, and their cellular payment, Apple Pay is authentic to that philosophy. There is not any app to download, and it works on iPhones, and may be used for on line purchases on Macs.

The consumer affords the credit score card statistics to their Apple account. Then the iPhone is used for the purchase via a contactless payment technique at a retail, and it is taken into consideration because the person has to verify identification thru the Touch ID sensor or Face ID. Users also can without difficulty ship coins thru an iMessage, or by simply asking Siri, the digital assistant. When you receive the coins, it goes for your Apple Pay Cash balance, which may be finally transferred on your financial institution account.

Apple Pay is widespread at approximately half of US retail places, along with the famous retail institutions of Starbucks, Walgreens, McDonald's and Best Buy among many others. When the usage of a debit card there's no fee, and for a credit score card there may be a 3% fee.

2. Google Pay

Widespread acceptance of preloaded on many Android phones needs different app a person's bills. The Android cell fee app is Google Pay which comes preloaded on Android smartphones. It is standard at many retail stores, such as Bloomingdale's, Chick-Fil-A, KFC, Nike and Staples, and additionally online services inclusive of Airbnb and Door Dash.

It claims to be easier than using a conventional credit store card as the card range is not immediately sent and protected through multi-layer safety encryption. Google Pay helps several credit score playing cards from some of the foremost providers, together with Chase, Citi, Discover and American Express.

However, there's a manner to directly connect your PayPal account, and Visa cards and are supported via Visa Checkout. Debit card payments are loose, and credit score payments incur a per cent rate.

Also confusing is the reality that for you to send cash without delay to every other user (person-to-character transaction), you want a unique app: Google Pay Send.

3. PayPal

A huge-name payment company, but watch the prices in some cases

It looks as if PayPal has been around for eons when it comes to on line transactions, and with their cellular app they need to move beyond just offering seller protection for eBay purchases.
These days, they supply direct person-to- person payments, and moreover, to get into the retail charge area, still more likely that it will pay on line with this service than at the checkout counter. This is due to the dearth of guide for NFC with PayPal's app, and best a handful of retailers leaping on the bandwagon to just accept PayPal has hampered efforts so far.

A disadvantage of PayPal has been the costs, which can be complex and hard to recognize as there are so a lot of them. At least for getting a product on-line or in-character, PayPal does not price a rate, nor does it rate for someone to switch (without seller protection).

However, at the same time as shifting from a linked financial institution account it does not incur a price, with an Instant Transfer from a related debit card, there is a $0.25 price in line with transfer (and by the way, it is not so instantaneous.

4. Venmo

The cash transferring associate to Facebook

Free for transactions without credit score card, connects to Facebook contacts, limited reputation at outlets. Venmo works through a mobile app on your phone and signing up can be performed with your Facebook account, in case you decide on it. Next, you hyperlink your bank account or credit card.

Then you can use the app to ship or acquire money from different Venmo customers, or you could ship cash thru a phone or e-mail because the app can get admission to your Facebook or phone contacts; and if the recipient is not presently on Venmo they are brought on to create an account.

Venmo is greater useful for online bills, however some outlets do take delivery of it. Receiving and sending cash are free, however there may be a 3% fee to be used of a credit score card.

5. Samsung Pay

A useful mobile payment app restrained to Samsung telephones.
High level of acceptance works at older magnetic strip terminals, limited range of supported phones.
Leveraging their market reach as the first-rate selling producer of Android smartphones, the electronics giant brings us their mobile charge providing, Samsung Pay.

It is supported on several of Samsung's contemporary flagship smartphones, including the Galaxy S9, but not on different producer's phones, limiting greater adoption. The Samsung Pay app connects to credit and debit cards from a number of foremost banks.

The desirable aspect about Samsung Pay is the close to universal recognition as merchants. Rather, Samsung Pay works with conventional credit card readers, the use of the more modern EMV or NFC tech, or maybe the older ones using magnetic strip era – by conserving the smartphone subsequent to it, the credit card facts contained inside the magnetic strip gets transmitted thru a generation called magnetic cosy transmission (MST).

With such flexibility in interacting with the credit score card reader, Samsung Pay can sincerely update that pile of credit score playing cards on your wallet with a phone app.

Mobile-simply social

Marketers and enterprise managers have now acknowledged the recognition—and the coming near power—of cellular- with the most effective being social apps. Establishing the right mobile cell presence on the social media platform giants like Facebook, Instagram, Twitter, and Tumblr is now a must have. Make certain you increase and drive particular strategies for each social media platform, to hold client and goal marketplace to assist engagement.

Diversify content material, however, make certain they all serve to support and support ones logo. This means you could put up the identical or comparable content(s) throughout your social media domain names, or specific ones—depending on your commercial enterprise and marketing needs and dreams. The key concerns here, however, are nevertheless logo identification and consumer engagement. When you satisfy these, in method you are generating effective cell content and making use of them nicely throughout structures.

Maximise on your specific strategies
Maximising to your precise mobile techniques need no longer be complex and tedious. Remember to simply use the proper and right key phrases to your content advertising. Focus and prioritise on unique offers and income.
Be sure your contact statistics is blanketed to your mobile sites and pages and are then easily reachable. And, be compatible with your current customers in addition to your target marketplace.

Be like minded in the way you have made certain all your websites and pages are without difficulty on hand through, now, perceivable mobile cell gadgets to be had to and/or utilized by your clients and goals in the market.
Ensure all your cell marketing modules, materials, and contents are well matched with all mobile cell gadgets. Continuously replace materials to ensure they may be also constantly well suited, and for that reason constantly effortlessly accessible.

Text/SMS advertising
Employing a text or SMS advertising approach as a support to your ordinary mobile cell marketing desires will even carry more value to your commercial enterprise, in addition to opportunities for financial gain. You can be surprised at how clean textual content/SMS marketing schemes are.

What you want to do is to design an opt-in marketing campaign or set of campaigns that allow your contemporary clients in addition to your current ones to sign on and get hold of special messages, different deals, notifications, signals, and rewards for joining stated campaign(s).
Utilise this platform to permit your clients to make greater numerous and specific movements for all that are beneficial for your mobile cell advertising desires, and consequently, to your enterprise.

These purchaser moves, range from participating in surveys or even just being redirected for your important website or focused pages. Make positive your praise to clients who frequently take part in your campaigns, and interact new members, too, so they maintain on joining your destiny campaigns.

When you understand that mobile marketing now is critical but different as a medium, one could effortlessly adapt and shift your marketing plans towards successfully harnessing all viable upsides out of the cellular marketing techniques. Doing so is ensuring you are live and up to date, however one is making sure one is in advance and on top of the opposition, and that your commercial enterprise flourishes.

M-trade area is wonderful for the installed e-trade area (Dholakia & Dholakia 2004). In essence, m-trade offers possibilities for contacting customers at more than one place, for personalizing offerings and offerings in sparkling ways and for making viable new types of services and purchasing stories (Samuelsson & Dholakia 2003).

This consists of programme improvement, service shipping and client care. In assessment, infrastructure and services consists of (a) mobile shipping that refers to the primary networks that permits cellular communications including transmission and switching for voice and records; (b) cell offerings and shipping support entails, for instance, the infrastructure in accessing the Internet, protection, the server platform and payment structures; (c) mobile interface and programs specializes in integrating the infrastructure and structures with customers, i.e. Hardware, software program and communications.

There are programs of wi-fi advertising including those based totally on quick-range wireless 'hotspots' and used, as an instance, in shopping departments, shops and street cafes for delivering advertising communications to the clients' cell phone. Undoubtedly, those programs may be used for advertising and marketing and advertising functions.

Figure: 3

Mobile Marketing Platform

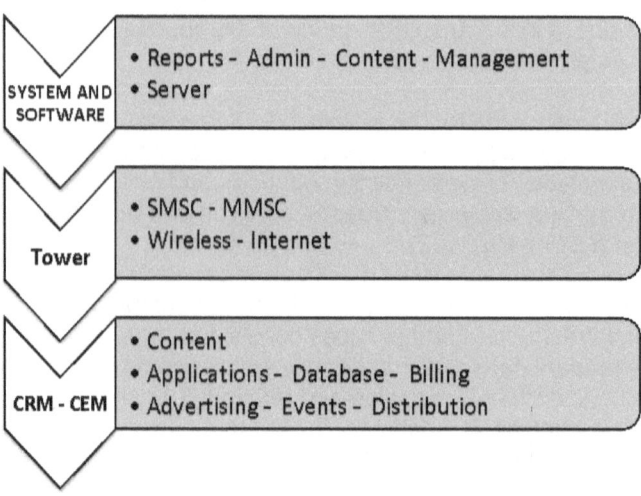

However, because of their constrained transmission variety, i.e. Wi-fi services enabled by WLAN technology can most effective attain customers located within a near bodily proximity of the wi-fi carrier company (Carnovsky & Harihar 2006), and therefore actual mobility can handiest b via an underlying mobile community, which implements the mobility across the whole region protected (Balasubramanian et al. 2002)

Over two decades, interactivity has been widely discussed in fields which include advertising and marketing, advertising, communique, statistics science, computer technology and schooling (McMillan & Hwang 2002). In his dialogue of technological traits facilitating communique, Rogers (1986) diagnosed growing interactivity as a key development and emphasised the need for research that would make a contribution to our knowledge of computer-mediated interactivity.

Computer-mediated interactivity can be labelled into large perspectives – medium (tool-centric) and message-centric perspectives (Yadav and Varadarajan 2005).

Specifically, medium perspectives provide insights into laptop-mediated-communique (CMC) gear, and message-centric views consciousness on analysing communication patterns facilitated by means of these mobile, communique equipment.

REVISION

- Using 120 words, as a mobile marketing expert describe what mobile

  solution (s) you would use working for a major supermarket chain.

- Based on your answer above, describe and explain the benefits of your

  strategy.

DEVELOPING A MOBILE MARKETING STRATEGY - 5

OBJECTIVES
Developing a mobile marketing strategy is the process of identifying how one will go about using MM in a given marketplace. Getting the strategy right is critical in achieving key objectives.

Chapter Learning Outcomes
- To comprehend the logic of MM
- To consider MM applications in marketing today
- An appreciation of MM benefits in a marketing context

Critical thinking
Having completed this topic, one will be able to:
- Appreciate the development of MM strategies and discuss it
- Have an appreciation of MM in marketing to date
- Be able to consider the future of MM in a business

Critical thinking
Having completed this topic, one will be able to:
- Discuss and debate MM strategy as a topic
- Analyse MM strategy material applications and understand it
- Consider MM application in a work setting

In the authors experience the place to start is understanding the customer who are they, where are they, what are they looking for and why are they looking for it. Once this information is known the marketing team can concentrate on developing the strategy for mobile marketing as well as completing the setting of KPI's and Metrics to measure performance. Critical in the analysis before a marketing Mobile campaign begins is the use of various scenarios to measure the return on investment of a range of Mobile marketing actions, this insures relevance to the Financial benefits of the campaign. In summary we are defining the objectives for mobile marketing as well as defining the target audience so that the mobile campaign is effective and is fully integrated.

So, what is the objective? Is it to get your leads or make sales, is it to build awareness or provide information on channels of distribution? Objectives or goals provide the marketing team needs to be precise in its objectives however the goals should be realistic and achievable.

A positive way to building objectives is to review case studies of Mobile campaigns those that have worked and those that failed.

Look at the target market and audience customer groups use different mediums to gain information, as smartphones increase in popularity the wider the usage band of age, income becomes less problematic.

Millennial's are big users of mobile devices and therefore Mobile marketing works well amongst this target group. Under 30-year-olds use mobiles more than over sixty –year-olds. The big question for mainly marketing teams is, does the mobile marketing audience match the standard target market for the company's products or services.

The only way to find out is to research build a framework of the consumer or buyer who uses Mobile devices.

In the research process ask questions about the psychographic characteristics of the target as well as key identification factors. Look for habits and values and what they consider are the pinch points in buying goods and services.

Google and Alexa have range of data on existing Mobile customers. Key point notes are that Mobile users also use the Internet and therefore your website is used to find information therefore is key to optimise the website co jointly with the mobile program.

According to Google/ Nielsen Mobile Path to purchase data, 48% customers start their research using search engines with 33% starting on branded websites with 26% using branded apps. Marketing teams must look upon mobile marketing as a different medium from other mass communication mediums.

A large portion of customers will not recommend to friends and family a website where the mobile experience has been poor, getting mobile content right drives responses and the mobile process must 'harmonise' with the website. The benefits of this action are:

- One code base

- Higher search rankings

- Increased site speed

- Future proof

- Decreased loaded time

- Functionality on all devices

- One universal URL

- Production of all screens sizes

- Clean and highly flexible grids and layouts

- Higher quality

It is clear that the integration of mobile and website insurers that consumers see a one sight one sound delivery of the brand message which strives to build key value propositions.

In material from Annalect (2018), smartphone owning millennials expectations from brands using technology 55% were looking for Mobile friendly websites or acts with 44% seeking some form of human interaction.

Figure 4.

Mobile Marketing Life Cycle

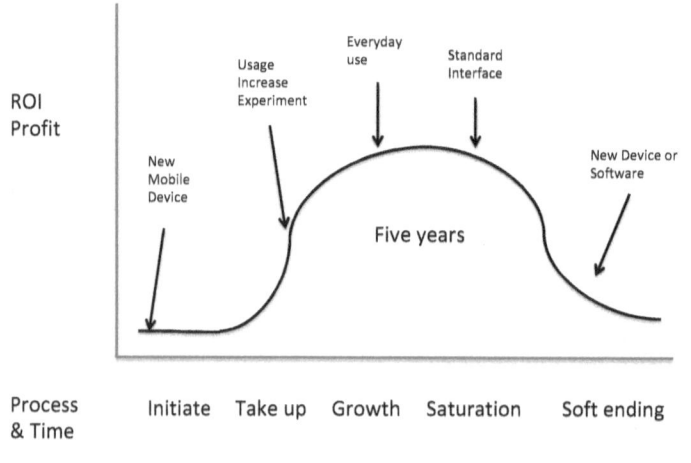

Copyright: James Seligman (2017)

The key objectives of mobile marketing are to obtain a good ROI and build profits for the organization. Mobile uses a process that alters in time as consumers become familiar with the use of a new mobile device, it takes time to appreciate how much a mobile phone for example can accomplish. In the initial stages the consumer is experimenting and exploring, becoming familiar with the device and its wide applications. Use equates to benefit and as take up grows through experimentation mobile users become accustomed to this time saving go anywhere tool.

The next stage is everyday use, "mobile device becomes indispensable in the authors view it becomes a close Buddy / Friend / Aid, Seligman (2017). However, as time goes by new innovation comes along and this mobile relationship, this standard interface, becomes stale and use drops off replaced with a bigger, better device some of which have not been invented."

One must remember Mobile phones are primarily used as a communication device amongst friends and family therefore the integration of mobile with social networks, content marketing and CRM and CEM insures a viable mobile program.

Overall mobile marketing enables a range of activities to be used that link with business and marketing strategy, it also should be recalled the mobile marketing effectiveness can vary by industry and sector.
Figure 5.

Mobile Environmental Influences

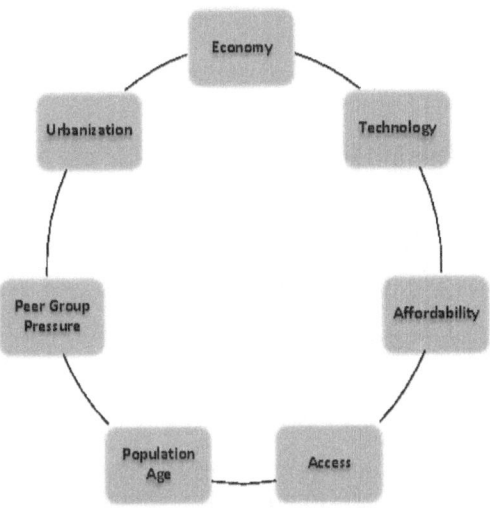

On a macro level there are range all environmental influences the marketing needs to consider when debating the use of the application of mobile, the first is the economy how advanced is it and does allow for mobile marketing applications, how good is the technologies in the market of choice as mobile depends on the quality of technology as a driver.

In emerging markets, the affordability of purchase of mobile device needs to be considered as well as the monthly fees as both influence the penetration and usage of mobile devices in any given marketplace. Look carefully at access to buy a mobile device and also consider the structure of the mobile infrastructure in the marketplace, as the capacity to obtain signal is critical.

A further consideration is the population age, mobiles are used more young people, and it is the fact the many markets have a mature population from the baby boomers of the 50's. Look carefully at statistics on the usage and penetration of mobile devices amongst older people.

Changes in lifestyle drives peer group pressure for consumers have the latest Mobile technology at their fingertips, a two year old iPhone, is no longer considered up-to-date and the pressure to upgrade from friends and family is strong.

Also, consider urbanisation in emerging markets where people are leaving the countryside to become city dwellers where there are more jobs and opportunities.

Look at the following carefully:

- Proximity

- Applications

- Location

- Apps available

- Use of in MMS and SMS

- Are coupons affective

- What search processes are available

- Could banners be used

With a higher knowledge of the drivers of mobile tools and offerings adoption and the role of mobile advertising in purchaser selection-making, marketers and entrepreneurs can increase a more powerful cellular advertising approach. The framework that Shankar, O'Driscoll, and Reibstein (2003) advise is useful in formulating an organizations mobile cell advertising method at a macro level.

The approach can be regarded alongside two dimensions: the degree of change to the commercial enterprise version, and the merit of organizational transformation required. Depending at the mixtures of the degrees of those dimensions, a company can adopt one in every of three standard mobile advertising strategies.

When both the need to exchange the enterprise model and the want for organizational transformation are low, then the company have to comply with the "operational overall performance" approach.

This approach involves the use of mobile media and communications for supply chain and workforce productiveness improvement. When the need to change the commercial enterprise model and the need for organizational change are at slight range, then the recommended strategy is a "attain and range" approach.

Initiatives under this approach consist of improving product/ provider range, improving loyalty, and increasing customer reach. When the need to change the enterprise version and the need for organizational transformation are high, then the firm ought to undertake a "new enterprise fashions" method.

Under this strategy, the firm fundamentally alters its shape and marketplace method, or adjustments the way it does enterprise to cope with competitive threats.

However in the authors view here is an easier alternative framework:

Figure 6.

Mobile Marketing Strategy

Level one   **CUSTOMER / TARGET**

RESEARCH – OBJECTIVES – PLAN – CUSTOMER – STRATEGY-ANALYTICS - ROI - RELEVANCE

KEY DECISIONS

Level two

MOBILE MARKETING PROCESSES

SEARCH – COUPONS – APPS – PROXIMITY – MMS / SMS – BANNERS – GEO FENCING – OFFERS – INTEGRATION WITH WEBSITE – BACK AND FRONT OFFICE

Copyright: (James Seligman,2017)

Level One starts with defining the customer or target for the goods or services using mobile marketing, this is usually achieved through robust analysis of the marketplace and competition, what has worked, what has failed. Follow this up with some really good research both qualitative and quantitative to really understand the customer and then needs and wants. This allows you to insert your objectives, what is it you want the mobile marketing program to achieve. Objectives should include Financial, share, sales, customer attitudes and opinions levels.
The planning process around the customer then moves into the strategy stage where the marketing team define exactly what they are going to do and why they're going to do it so that the return on investment is positive. The setting of

KPI's and metric measures provides the marketing team with the tools to determine the mobile marketing campaigns success or otherwise.

In this level one process the marketing team needs to understand the relevance all the mobile marketing program within the context of the broader marketing activity of the organization and ensure the mobile marketing program is fully integrated to maximize communication effectiveness and return on investment.

Level two takes into consideration level one and concerns itself with the right makes of mobile marketing tools that will maximize the mobile marketing budget and gain the best returns
.

Many people have asked, what is the right strategy to use, there is no one answer, in industry sectors, competition influences the best contextual way of developing an effective Mobile marketing program. So how does one choose the right mobile marketing tools?

Look at the industry and consider best practice. Moreover, rely on your research to guide you into the right tools bearing in mind budget and also return on investment objectives. In many cases, it is about trial and error. What we know is that mobile marketing works if executed well.

Look at the following carefully (Seligman, 2017):
- Location

- Tools

- Access

- Apps choice

- Use of in MMS and SMS, best choice decision

- Are incentives affective

- What consumer search processes are available

- Could banners be used efficiently

Figure 7.

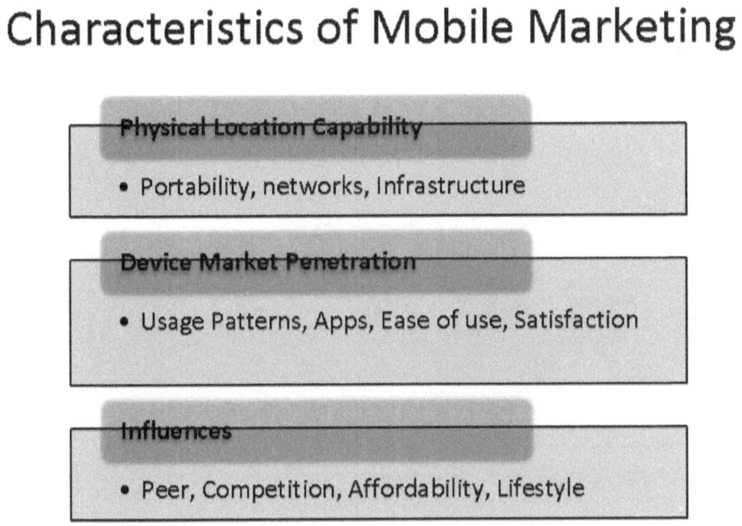

Characteristics of Mobile Marketing

Physical Location Capability

- Portability, networks, Infrastructure

Device Market Penetration

- Usage Patterns, Apps, Ease of use, Satisfaction

Influences

- Peer, Competition, Affordability, Lifestyle

Copyright: James Seligman (2017)

The characteristics of mobile marketing comes down to three influencing factors (Seligman, 2017) they are identified in the chart above " one the characteristics of effective mobile marketing is physical location capability, in other words how close can the message be delivered to the consumer that will influence the purchase

This is despite the device market penetration which is vital as without good distribution of mobile devices is the primary prerequisite for an effective mobile marketing campaign.

In most mature markets there are existing influences that has driven mobile device purchase and usage one of them is social networks which allowed communication amongst like-minded people."

Figure 8.

Implication of Mobile in Strategy

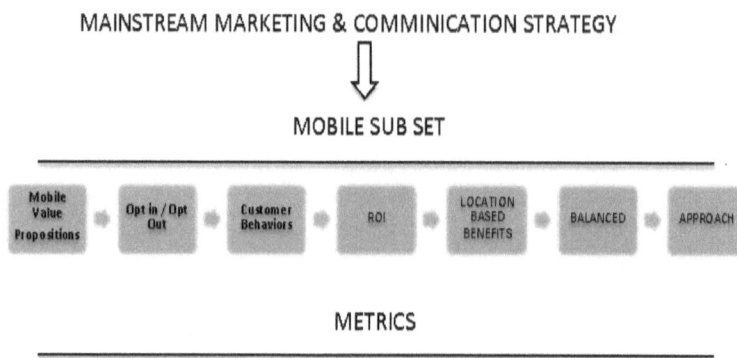

MAINSTREAM MARKETING & COMMINICATION STRATEGY

MOBILE SUB SET

Mobile Value Propositions → Opt in / Opt Out → Customer Behaviors → ROI → LOCATION BASED BENEFITS → BALANCED → APPROACH

METRICS

REACH - FREQUENCY - IMPACT - SHARE - EXPERIENCE - PROPENSITY - ROI

"In any enterprise mainstream marketing and communication needs a strategy on which a choice can be made to use mobile as a subset to maximize an organizations capability to reach on the move consumers. When looking at mobile, consider, are the primary value propositions the same for mobile, do they need shortening, changing to fit the medium.

Look at opt in and out, this is a critical decision and depends on the sector of business and products and services offered. How do customers behave, would they respond well to mobile messages and use the medium to purchase, which drives ones return on investment.

If one has bricks and mortar outlets, e-commerce what benefits would a mobile program bring, recall geo fencing as a tool that could attract business locally. Also, with e-commerce, a mobile message of 'get 20% off in the next 20 minutes at www…. is a powerful incentive.

Be balanced in ones approach to mobile, and ensure the offer fits the product or service one provides, as success or otherwise should be measured like any other marketing investment," Seligman (2017).

Once a company formulates an appropriate mobile advertising and marketing method, it needs to pick out appropriate cellular advertising method, which should be consistent with the chosen strategy. Mobile advertising or mobile marketing methods consist of text messaging, integrated content, games, interactive voice response, wireless access protocol (WAP) websites, ring-tones and ring-back tones, viral, geo-targeting, mobile broadcast advertising, cell smartphone sponsorships, and cellular telemarketing.

Figure 9.

MOBILE MARKETING STRATEGY OPTIONS

Copyright: James Seligman (2017)

Text messaging, the maximum popular mobile advertising approach, it is useful for sweepstakes, contest balloting, and right away redeemable. The predominant upsides of text messaging are that it is simple for both the marketer and the consumer, measurable, and has excessive reaction and conversion costs.

Mobile Telemarketing additionally has favourable reaction amongst individuals who decide to use it, but if the incorrect message is introduced to the wrong person at the wrong time, it can incur the annoyance of clients, service and government.

In selecting the mobile marketing methods to apply for a campaign, mobile marketers and entrepreneurs need to: Seligman (2018).

(1) "Make assessment of the pros and cons of each method

(2) Estimate the synergies a number of the methods

3) Review the mobile methods utilized successfully by competitors."
Both enterprise-to-patron (B2C) and business-to-commercial enterprise (B2B) marketers use these mobile advertising and marketing methods (Shankar and Hollinger 2007).

In the B2C space, Johnson & Johnson uses textual content messaging for its optical merchandise. A poster asks optometry patients with cellular gadgets to type in "MYEYE" whilst they wait on the optician's or the optometrist's office.

J&J then sends a reminder message or/and promotional message about its products when the affected person is within the health practitioner's workplace (Cuno 2005). In the B2B area, Federal Express (FedEx) uses the text messaging and geotargeting techniques synergistically. It sends messages to commercial enterprise executives who have chosen to get hold of FedEx message approximately record offerings while they're close to a FedEx Kinko's area.

Whereas a sound mobile advertising and marketing strategy pursued with appropriate methods may be powerful, only a few organisations will rely totally on mobile marketing. Rather, mobile advertising can be an effective supplement to different advertising methods of a company, and an alternative choice a confined set of those activities. Accordingly, it seems that mobile advertising greatly suits the "attain and variety" approach.

The key advertising choices for a mobile marketing strategy include the ones on marketing communication (marketing and sales advertising), delivery of digital products and services, and customer relation control (customer service and guide).

At a high level, some of questions remain unresolved in the context of a firm's mobile advertising method. A principal problem relates to how the company's mobile strategy meshes with the firm's common marketing approach. In this context the question to ask is, 'how ought to the cell method supplement or alternative elements of the company's overall advertising and marketing approach?'

Specifically, how do the advertising and marketing campaigns be redesigned to encompass a mobile program, and how should that element hyperlink to tasks in mass media or at the Internet?

Mobile marketing can be related to economies of scope on this context, in which case it may expand ordinary advertising and marketing efficiency and effectiveness. For example, client reaction can also improve drastically if mobile advertising campaigns are pursued in coordination with email and/or direct mail campaigns while they are uncoordinated.

Furthermore, how ought a company's mobile advertising approach evolve across (a) the product life cycle, and (b) the consumer lifestyles cycle? These questions advocate that there are adequate studies and opportunities associated with the development and execution of a mobile marketing method strategy. Here are some author points on areas which may assist one calibrate a mobile approach.

Figure 10.

Mobile Considerations

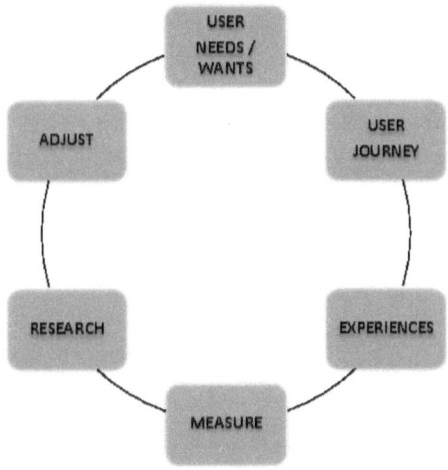

Copyright: James Seligman (2017)

REVISION
- In 50 words define the importance of consumer research in MM

- Using 150 words outline the importance of harmonising MM processes with a web site.

TYPES OF MOBILE STRATEGIES -6

OBJECTIVES
MM has many possible strategy scenarios; how do you pick the right mix to maximize ROI?

Chapter Learning Outcomes
- To comprehend the various strategy options in MM
- To understand each MM application in marketing today
- An appreciation of MM tools in a marketing context

Critical thinking
Having completed this topic, one will be able to:
- Appreciate the strategic development of MM action and discuss it
- Have an appreciation of MM options marketing to date
- Be able to consider the outcomes of MM and ROI

Critical thinking
Having completed this topic, one will be able to:
- Discuss and debate MM strategy options as a topic
- Analyse MM strategy material and understand it
- Consider MM application in a work setting

1.Text SMS Promotions

These are usually campaigns advertised off line and when customers are on the move, which promotes the use of text by using a key word or short code to receive the offer. What are the policies and best practices for SMS advertising and marketing? (Textmarketer.co.uk, 2017)
Make sure your contacts have opted in.
Text messaging is a powerful and direct line of verbal exchange to the consumer. But there are numerous regulations which you must consider whilst making plans for your SMS advertising approach.

The first, and maximum critical of these is receiving permission out of your contacts to send them SMS messages. Be aware of the timing of your messages. Unlike e mail, which is best checked a few instances every day (at maximum), consumers open text messages almost at once. This is splendid for urgent messages however you do not need to abuse this by way of stressful contacts at unusual hours within the day.

Would you need to run out and use a discount that just woke you up at 2 AM on a Wednesday night? Some nations even have legal guidelines about whilst you could ship advertising textual content messages (e.g. France does not allow SMS advertising on Sundays, holidays, or each time after 10 PM).

Include your organisation's name in your messages.

When sending bulk SMS messages, most carriers send them through a short code, which means your contacts will not know it is coming from you. That is why you have to let your contacts recognise who is sending the message inside the first area. Use SMS to complement the rest of your virtual advertising method.

The splendour of digital advertising and marketing is that there are such a lot of channels that you may use to have interaction together with your clients.
All these channels tie together to create an advertising and marketing communication device that allows agencies to build relationships with clients and leads at remarkable scale.

SMS and e mail advertising are channels which might be very complementary. You can create campaigns via both channels, using mail together with greater exact facts and SMS to talk greater time-sensitive or pressing facts.

2. Mobile Coupons
The coupon is sent directly to the customer who in turn using email messages that are redeemed at retail. Mobile couponing takes many forms, each with strengths and obstacles, mmaglobal.com,(2018). In maximum instances, a cellular coupon itself is not a real coupon, but as an alternative a promotional communique displayed at the consumer's cellular device. Mobile coupon kinds, range from:

- A simple textual content message alert offering reductions and

  promotions

- A uniquely coded offer that requires validation at point of sale

- An alert containing a link to an advertiser's promotional provide

- A cellular coupon tied to a retailer's loyalty software

Text-message alerts
The best form of a cellular "coupon" is a primary textual content-message alert that simply communicates a suggestion. For example, "Receive 10 per cent off all flat-screen TVs. This weekend only." Such promotions, of direction, are available to all clients.

However, clients who opt-in improve the success of the merchandising, because an alert is focused, and offers brought incentive for customers.

Another advantage of textual content-alert campaigns: They reach a mass-marketplace audience across definitely all telephones and are rather easy to execute. In addition, clients can choose in for periodic alerts thru the advertisers' conventional media.

Mobile promotions confirmed at point of sale
Advertisers regularly want to offer precise promotions to pick out customers through a traditional coupon. In this example, purchasers who opt-in to acquire cell promotions get the offer. Consumers display the offer on their phones at the factor of sale, validating their bargain or advertising.

Mobile messages can also include a unique code that can be entered at the check in. These codes permit advertisers to confirm the promotion and shield towards consumers reusing the coupon offer.

Beyond the boundaries of text-based coupons

The problem with text-based cellular coupons: They include just that -- simplest textual content. Moreover, wi-fi companies limit the scale of each text message to 160 characters - definitely much less, given characters required for disclaimers.

Furthermore, a textual content message cannot accommodate UCC and EAN bar codes, nor include a completely unique or impactful image.

MMS-primarily based mobile coupons
In comparison, mobile alerts may be added to customers through an MMS (Multimedia Messaging Service),that could contain multimedia objects together with photos, audio, video and rich text. While greater graphically than simple text, an MMS transmission is lots more costly to supply than textual content messages. (Imagine a 50-cent coupon that expenses 20 cents for the advertiser to ship and 10 cents for the purchaser to receive.)

An MMS can consist of pictures of UPC bar codes, but the images cannot be appropriately scanned through most point-of-sale scanning gadgets, preventing tracking and measurement.

Mobile cell phone scanning snags
If POS scanning gadgets fail to read the code on a cellular cell phone display, the cashier must manually enter each, the UPC and the cut price offer code without delay into the sign in. However, manual access of codes is less than perfect.

Mobile hyperlinks to coupons
A low-budget opportunity exists to MMS couponing with considerable advantages to the advertiser. A mobile textual content message may be despatched with a hyperlink that, whilst selected, opens to a page with a discount image (as an instance, "£25 off for new clients").

The landing page's layout can incorporate rich gadgets, shades and sort patterns, turning in an extra eye-attractive and powerful mobile coupon than just text.

The tracking code can be made less difficult to read than SMS textual content. And after a given expiration date, the coupon can disappear from the client's mobile telephone.

Coupons within branded cellular programs
A cellular coupon can be packaged as a characteristic inside a store's mobile Internet (WAP) website online or downloadable handset-resident utility.
The coupon appears as one among numerous menu alternatives. For example, WAP web sites and applets might display a menu item such as "Alerts and Coupons" -- as shown inside the cellular website -- or "What's on today."

Consumers who click on "Alerts and Coupons" can opt in to obtain periodic textual content messages for store specials, promotions and bargain gives.

The textual content message consists of a hyperlink that returns the consumer to the WAP website, where the coupon is displayed. This technique encourages common use of the advertiser's cellular app.

Coupons delivered inside a mobile software deliver advertisers the ability to track and seize the behaviour of clients.

They recognize, for instance, how frequently precise offers are regarded and how many are forwarded to friends. In addition, a few mobile providers can target the conduct of specific clients and provide their clients with information for segmentation and targeting.

Advertisers must determine what coupon sorts to offer within their cell programs. For example, does a client in reality display his or her mobile coupon to a shop clerk or does a tracking code need to be captured for redemption? If purchasers simplest need to display their coupons at point of buy, what is to stop them from the use of a discount numerous times to obtain a couple of reductions or offers?
Mobile apps exists that allows advertisers to set the variety of instances each coupon may be opened -- say no extra than two occurrences before it expires -- actually disappears.

Mobile coupons connected to loyalty cards
Most coupon advertising nowadays nevertheless requires the gathering of a real paper coupon. The purpose: a paper coupon, revealed with its specific codes, is essential for financial reconciliation of trade-value agreements. Therefore, the usage of paper coupons will preserve, especially inside the grocery enterprise. Nevertheless, mobile coupon campaigns can nonetheless be implemented successfully.

These campaigns combine the cellular merchandising with the grocery store's loyalty card program.

Consumers sign in to receive reductions and promotions offered in the marketer's mobile application. Consumers actually input their loyalty card ID into the mobile software once.

This movement efficaciously ties the cellular software to the store's loyalty program. From this point forward, purchasers obtain automated discounts at the sign in once they use their loyalty card.

Because the patron has registered for the cut price, the marketer can then send cell signals to the customer's phone that announce new discounts. Retailers emerge as proponents of those cell packages, due to the fact that they provide a further incentive to use loyalty cards and pressure store visitors.

A common mobile application situation for retailing:
Step 1. The items enterprise promotes its mobile software on in-store displays and other demonstration collateral (theappsolutions.com,2018).

The advertising encourages clients to use their telephones to register their retailer loyalty card quantity within the cell software that allows you to:

- Obtain automatic discounts at the check in, and
- Receive text-message signals of shop discounts

(When a consumer enters his or her loyalty card wide variety, the mobile software updates the store's loyalty software database, which flip triggers shop registers to bargain products from companies imparting rate reductions.)

Step 2. The enterprise sends a text message to customers' phones, alerting them of a discount campaign, and explaining that the usage of the shop's loyalty card at check-out will routinely apply the cut price.

Step 3. Consumers, incentivised by means of the mobile alert, input the shop and select from the shelf the items promoted on their phone. They proceed to checkout and, upon providing their loyalty card, acquire the fee reductions.

How will consumers discover your cell coupons?
How can shops and brands promote cell reductions and promotional gives together with their mobile packages?

For mass-market reach, they could acquire cell commonplace brief codes (five-digit telephone numbers) and keywords and use them in traditional media (print commercials, out of home, radio and television).

Also, brief codes can appear in catalogues and Web sites, posters, store circulars and unsolicited mail.

In addition, in-shop sales staff can be trained to acquire customers' cell smartphone numbers at checkout, indicating that the smartphone quantity may be used to send most effective occasional text messages on discounts, coupons, new merchandise and occasions.

It is important to send an opt-in text message confirming the purchasers' interest to take part.

This message can also consist of a hyperlink to a branded mobile application, presenting unfastened software of strong hobby to subscribers, similarly to the coupons.

What to offer?
Many offers can be supplied within your cell application, among them: charge reduction; free products; purchase-one-get-one unfastened; time release (coupons, disbursed together, that have special expiration dates, encouraging repeat purchases); crossruff (the customer receives a discount for one product, regularly related, when purchasing another); sweepstakes entry redeemable simplest at specification shops or places; and ordinary (a producer distributes a discount suitable on a couple of products).

Although mobile couponing, in its various forms, will not make paper coupons extinct right away, coupons on cellular telephones will continue to flourish.

Mobile coupon benefits

- Increase shop site visitors and Net Outside Sales (NOS)

- Deepen brand loyalty and inspire return visits on your mobile presence

  -- via text alerts and in-utility gives that alternate frequently

- Encourage use of save loyalty cards using cellular coupons as a brand

  new consumer-acquisition and retention channel

- Promote products primarily based on consumers' behaviour inside a

  firm's mobile software

- Gain a database of opt-in mobile numbers

3. Mobile payment

This is a service that provides elements of value to the customer in retail locations who are connected to POS or m-commerce. Mobile payments cover any payment made using a cellular tool, Roberts (2018). Due to our ever-increasing smartphone dependence, various methods have been developed to allow consumers to pay effortlessly through a cell phone.

To place this in context, information displays that a third of UK clients are actually using their NFC-enabled telephones for contactless payments in shops.
Apple Pay, with their 'limitless' transactions, has even brought about a 11% increase in the average mobile transaction overall within the remaining 1/2 of 2017, as increasingly customers experience using their smartphones for point-of-sale transactions.

But there are extra forms of cellular payments than contactless telephone bills, both for far off, or face-to-face payments. Let's study the exceptional ways you may pay with a cellular phone.

Point-of-sale answers
- Near-field verbal exchange (NFC) bills

Use of near-field conversation (NFC) bills is growing rapidly within the UK. Digital wallets and the use of NFC for contactless card machines consist of Apple Pay, Samsung Pay and Google Pay. But how does it work?

NFC phones speak with NFC-enabled card machines the usage of near-proximity radio frequency identification. The mobile phones do not contact the pad factor at sale to switch records, i.e. Cash, but they must be within some inches of the terminal.

In London, busses and tube stations utilise telephone bills through NFC in which you will generally tap the tour card. Similarly in China, NFC is typical as a means of fee on all public delivery, and in Japan, it is also getting used to offer identification card facts. In Nice, traffic and residents can use NFC to purchase almost something. NFC includes an immediate, nearly instantaneous transfer of encrypted statistics to point-of-sale devices, rather than chip and PIN generation that takes longer to method. Many cell telephone operators are searching at ways to similarly broaden this era.

Sound waves-based payments
Sound wave-based totally (or sound sign-based totally) cell bills constitute a more recent, current answer that works for many cell telephones.
Transactions are processed – without the want for internet – thru particular sound waves containing encrypted information approximately the price.

Sound waves are despatched from a terminal to the cell telephone to carry charge info, in which after the patron's smartphone converts that information into analogue alerts that finalise the transaction.

Instead of using inbuilt generation like NFC, your cell wallet, banking app or card terminal just requires an easy software program installation. There's no need for any greater hardware. This makes it a low-cost answer especially in areas and international locations in which human beings cannot come up with the money for the modern-day smartphones, however, rely upon more fundamental generation to manner bills.

Magnetic relaxed transmission (MST) bills
A third way to pay with a cellular smartphone at a card terminal is thru magnetic secure transmission (MST). Samsung Pay makes use of both MST and NFC payments for contactless mobile cell phone payments.

MST is when a telephone emits a magnetic sign imitating the magnetic strip at the payer's credit score card, which the card terminal selects up and processes as if a physical card become swiped via the machine.

Some card machines may also require a software replace to simply accept MST, but most new terminals be given it already.

Magnetic secure transmission is safe as NFC, in element due to the fact they both use a tokenisation gadget, and it is safer than the usage of a physically gift card.

Both in-retail and remote bills

Mobile wallets
A cell wallet (also referred to as digital wallet) shops fee records on a cell tool, commonly in an app. Mobile wallets, can utilise exclusive technologies within the price procedure, most often NFC, however different modalities like QR codes had been utilized by a few services.

Apple Pay is an instance that cuts across numerous categories, permitting contactless bills on card terminals (the usage of fingerprint authentication thru the smartphone), in-app purchases and bills at the net. Google Pay and Samsung Pay are other big cell wallet contenders.

Digital wallets are very secure to use. They generally work thru complex encryption and tokenisation, a method the use of time-restricted token numbers generated to technique the particular transaction using your already-encrypted card "stored" in your cell pockets.

Apart from credit score and debit pay cards, it's also viable to connect loyalty cards, boarding passes, tickets and different vital files in mobile wallets.

Quick response (QR) code payments

QR (abbreviation of "brief reaction") codes have many uses and are regularly located in advertising, on product labels and what seem to be the most random places.

Not every person knows they can be used to pay for goods too. It works via positive banking apps wherein you're playing cards are already related, and other apps with the aid of shops and vendors in which your card details can be related.

To use an example of in-store payments thru a QR code, supermarkets clients can use the Pay app, wherein their payment approach is hooked up, and virtually pay in retail through scanning a QR code at checkout through the app.

In all cases, you need to aim the Digi cam carefully to match the indicators for your smartphone display before the app can test the code. Some groups file feeling this is a hassle, mainly due to the fact you have first open the relevant app before you can start scanning.

Some e-trade organizations use QR codes at their internet site checkout as an opportunity to manually getting into card details.

For card-no longer-gift transactions, this is more secure because your telephone, that your card info are securely linked to, confirms you are the owner of the card – and due to the fact you are no longer typing your unencrypted card details on a device display.

Remote payments

Internet payments

Many groups pay on the internet of their telephone browser (e.g. Safari, Chrome) or inside apps, provided there is Wi-Fi or a 3G/4G network sign. There are numerous methods to pay this manner. For instance, you may manually enter card information on a website to pay for an order (just like on a computer), routinely use a financial institution card attached to a mobile app, use PayPal or comply with a hyperlink to a digital bill emailed to you.

Pre-2010, this became commonly known as wi-fi application protocol (WAP) payments. WAP used to be the maximum commonplace facility on smartphones connecting to the net.

So as opposed to a web browser with entry to the complete, people paid via an extra confined-potential WAP browser or app – collectively classed as WAP bills.

But instances have changed the pay panorama, and now, phones usually use a more recent mark-up language with complete right of entry to the internet.

SMS payments

SMS payments – also called SMS means deciding to buy products or services thru a text message. Once you have submitted a textual content message with the relevant statistics to the proper payee telephone variety, the charge amount is brought for your cellular phone invoice.

So, in impact, you are paying through your smartphone network company, perhaps via direct debit or pay-as-you-go – the manner you commonly pay to your smartphone use.

Just a few years ago, SMS payments had been one of the famous techniques of using mobile phones to pay for goods or services or donate to charity, due to its simplicity – all the user needs is a smartphone with textual content capability and pay as you go SIM card or telephone contract.

Direct carrier billing
Direct carrier billing (DCB) – additionally referred to as direct operator billing – is a manner to pay via your cellular service in preference to the use of bank or card details.

A manner to do this is to enter your smartphone number on a fee page or in an app, where once you undergo a few authentication steps to affirm you're the owner of that device (for example, by using confirming a textual content message). The charge will then be deducted out of your smartphone invoice or pay as you go SIM card as with SMS bills.

Digital offerings like Google Play and the App Store provide the option to pay by means of DCB. It is likewise used for TV voting, charity donations and subscriptions for virtual content.

Mobile banking
In some nations together with Sweden and the United Kingdom, cell banking has proven famous for transferring cash among private people or paying payments.

Mobile banking is clearly an app supplied by using the user's bank, through which you may conduct monetary transactions at once out of your financial institution account. This is commonly used for peer-to-peer transfers and payments to different people, but bills also can be paid this manner.

Each bank has their own sign-up methods for their app to verify you are the proprietor of the bank account.
 But as soon as signed up, it is also easy to log in in your cell phone and view your account balance and transaction records, make financial institution transfers. Every bank has their personal limits for what you could do through the app.

 4. Mobile display advertising
This mobile media adopts the use of search, mobile apps, social networks, and mobile publisher sites. Modern technological tendencies try to revolutionize the way in which facts are shared, Braux (2015). Different fields

are expected to benefit notably from these technological changes. One of those fields is that of advertising and marketing. Contemporary techniques of advertisement have made it feasible for each small and large agency to recognise their potentials. These commercial avenues have been vital for the economic survival and achievement of many companies.

Mobile Display Advertising, a present-day equivalent of cutting-edge methods of advertising, is becoming an established shape of advertising and because of its wholesome natural model it could end up a larger advertising and marketing discipline than SEO/SEA.

For many years, marketers have used both search engine optimization and SEA to recognize their business potentials. Companies and marketers that the usage of those forms of advertising have recorded good sized effects.

However, these advertising disciplines are presently associated with some of barriers that advise a brand-new shift to better avenues. Mainly due to the fact advertisers find it more and more difficult to create a nice response of investment.

Search engine marketing is also related to numerous limitations. Search engine marketing when taken into consideration is profitable but has its limits in phrases of advertising budget range that can be allocated for search engine results (upgrades in rankings).

It has taken into consideration a protracted-tail advertising-field and investments made, which takes a long time to return within the shape of sales. Simply placed: search engine optimization has its limits and is hard to scale.

With these problems in place, experts have been focusing on new marketing strategies and disciplines with the intention to supply superb effects. One of the new options, gaining worldwide traction, is Mobile Display Advertising (MDA). In the past, MDA has turn out to be greater and obvious as SEA/SEO. Many cases and research recommend that, over all, ROI's are good. However, a detailed evaluation indicates conclusively that Mobile Display Advertising continues to be unknown to many advertisers and entrepreneurs whilst it's taken into consideration a scalable model is needed to compete.

Mobile display has earned a main percentage of interest due to its increasing virtual spend – estimates vary but 2018 is going to pinnacle a hundred billion plus (numerous analyses show). Despite the truth that cell advertising is seen as a primary challenge with the aid of many marketers; specifically, because of its complexity at the start, MDA spends has been growing rapidly.

With this kind of boom, the environment has come up with both demanding situations and possibilities.

The opportunities associated with centred mobile show campaigns provide an explanation for why entrepreneurs should be prepared to seize the opportunity. There is a big amount of mobile stock, this is because everyone within the global market is on their smartphone all the time. This means customers are journeying websites and apps. In those apps and sites can be marketed.

There are various formats and creative technology that outline the modern-day mobile platform. The proliferation of mobile display formats has emerged thereby growing actionable commercials and with that, new possibilities. The marketplace is turning into professionals' agencies specialise in making reasonably-priced expert banners which are fine for customers. Many specialists encourage entrepreneurs to create cell-targeted banners that help a nice user experience. From video-banners to expandable formats, the MDA market is evolving unexpectedly.

It is also great that a few mobile advertising and marketing equipment have numerous obstacles. Some tools such as beacon technology had been characterized via numerous demanding situations.

This is the case due to the fact Beacon era is primarily based on an Opt-in version. Pop-up commercials have (f.e.) their limitations due to the fact the purchaser needs to have downloaded the app in query to acquire them.

Many publishers (e.g. Information businesses) have created mobile apps which could distribute the content material to greater visitors. Within those apps items may be marketed. These banners have the capability to create room for numerous interactions and communications.

Some of the banners have the potential to provoke on the spot messages or smartphone calls. Rich media advertisements are custom designed depending at the desires of the advertiser. Another tactic related to the MDA concept is the use of expendables. These codecs may be taken into consideration due to the fact action is needed to view the overall ad.

Real-time-bidding (RTB) is a quite new business mechanism whereby advertising stock is bought based on a per-impression foundation in an auction model. Bidding takes place real-time thereby making it feasible for the purchaser's advert to be displayed right away at the internet site. This form of MDA is received plenty attention due to its numerous (targeting) opportunities. Demand-aspect platforms (DSP) are systems that make it feasible for advertisers to manage statistics and a couple of exchange accounts through a single interface.

The number of cellular apps and websites allowing commercials in their content material is a brand new wave characterizing the sector of advertising. Such structures make it feasible for extra site visitors of the mobile web sites and users of particular apps to grow. Social media is (logically) additionally broadly a gift on mobile devices.

Facebook is currently being utilized by billions of people in extraordinary parts of the world. The visitation by people of apps and cell websites account form a big part of mobile visitors.

Mobile Display Advertising is easy, scalable and organic marketing model which makes use of this massive number of cellular visitors. In this 'scalable' and 'natural' confer with a version that has been around for decades if not centuries. Advertising in a newspaper or on television wishes a writer to hold that advertisement. For a newspaper for example, advertisements continue to be the biggest shape of revenue. MDA can be described as the current equivalent of advertising in newspapers or on TV.

Simply due to the truth that billions of people visit and use apps and cell web sites which can be owned by means of, let us say; publishers (whom want to be profitable).
MDA is a powerful version able to re-working, mobile advertising and marketing. It can be described as organic model as it is feasible and scalable for advertisers, it generates sales for publishers and legal limitations appear small.

The MDA version is wholesome and has the ability to convert the performance of many agencies. Research and the obvious growth of MDA suggests that it becomes a bigger marketing tool than SEA and search engine optimization are presently taken into consideration.

5. Mobile optimised website
This is the use of a website that has been especially developed so that the content is easy to access, very usable and therefore of value to customers connected via a mobile device (Zindigat.com, 2018).

Mobile optimization is the procedure of making sure that traffic having access to your website from mobile devices have an engaging and consumer-friendly to enjoy that has been optimized for that specific tool.

For example, while you cruise over to Amazon, the web site may be purposeful and smooth-to-use whether or not you are on your PC, your iPad, Android cell phone or another viable entry point.

The savvy people over at Amazon need to make certain the web site is cell optimized, in order that they do not miss a sale.

Is That the Same as Mobile-Friendly?

No. A mobile-pleasant site will reduce the dimensions of the pages of the website online to be viewable on mobile, however it is not be optimized or designed in a way that drives mobile conversions.

An optimized website online presents bigger navigation buttons, reformatted content material, and optimized snap shots so one can see the website online identifies that the consumer is on a mobile device.

Here is a countdown of reasons why one makes mobile optimization is a primary priority whilst we construct web sites for our customers:

1. Everyone is on Mobile. 1.2 billion individuals are using the web from their mobile gadgets. Additionally, eighty per cent of all net users are the users of a telephone. That is a lot of mobile site visitors that can be converted into leads for an enterprise.

2. Mobile Users Act Differently. Even though they will be restricted via facts, mobile users are ingesting visible media like crazy, and that they achieve this frequently through movies and pix. Having specific viewing behaviour creates yet some other possibility to interact ability customers on their computer.

3. Tablets are Money-Making Machines. Did you know that tablet users account for the highest common transaction than another device? And yes, that consists of desktops. So, for those who rely on e-Commerce income, you probably cannot afford for NOT to be optimized for mobile.

4. Landing Page Conversions. Landing pages on cellular need to be one of a kind versus your computer, so an internet site needs to accommodate this with pages that have a clean design, clear call-to-motion and a first-rate speedy load time. Not following mobile landing page high-quality practices may be an expensive danger when it comes to cellular conversion.

5. Because of Google. Google now palms out some consequences for any websites failing to full fill their requirements for cellular optimization. And as all of us have to realize, your commercial enterprise wishes to be buddies with Google.

In a nutshell, that is why one places inside the many hours of designing web sites a good way to work across all platforms and gadgets.
It is no longer a smooth job; however, one must take pride in ensuring customers accomplish inbound success through phone, tablet, pc, Surface or i-items.

6. Location based promotions

The concept recognises that customers will be at a certain location by sending them notices via the Mobile. The event is usually for entertainment or a reward. Location-based services (LBS) use real-time geographical facts from a mobile tool to provide information, enjoyment and security. Location-primarily based advertising (LBM) is one of the place-based total service.

Location-based advertising is a 'right away' advertising method that uses tool's and geo-statistics to alert the users approximately the offerings of organizations relevant to their location.

Snapchat CTA for Uber and LYFT

For example, Ridesharing apps like Uber and LYFT, use the tagged location in Snapchat to sell their transportation offerings. Snapchat gives an in-app call-to-action (CTA) for its users to e-book an Uber/LYFT journey to the vicinity tagged in the photograph that they are viewing. What is the difference between place-based advertising and marketing and area-based promoting? Location-primarily based advertising and marketing and region-based promotions are the subdomains of location-primarily based advertising and marketing. Location-based marketing is completed to build brand awareness, whereas place-primarily based promotion is used to push short-term income.

What is "radius targeting"?
Radius targeting, also known as proximity targeting, it is a vicinity-based advertising technology that permits businesses to target the consumers within the radius around a selected region. Radius targeted advertising is accomplished using technologies like GPS, RFID, NFC and Beacon Albright,(2017).

Let us say you have got a hotel near the airport. You may want to run radius focused campaigns at the airport for the provision of rooms. Passengers who overlooked a connecting flight or got re-routed due to weather situations would possibly discover these campaigns useful.

What is the difference between geo fencing and proximity marketing?

Geo fencing is one of the radius targeting strategies, that use GPS and/or RFID to create a digital fence across the area. Ads are then shown to customers who input that geo fence. Geo fencing is particularly helpful when you want to goal huge regions starting from over 50,000 meters to something less. It is beneficial for attracting clients however marketers need a greater accurate way to target customers in-store where messages should be extraordinarily contextual and applicable.

For a greater customized communique, marketers rely on proximity advertising. It is recommended to opt for proximity marketing for target regions ranging from 10 meters to three hundred meters.

Proximity marketing can be done via technology consisting of RFID, NFC, QR codes and Bluetooth beacons. Each era has its very own set of skills and boundaries.

However, given the maximum proximity use-cases, Bluetooth beacon generation is the most flexible and most effective proximity marketing technology.

What is the distinction between area-primarily based advertising and proximity advertising?

Proximity marketing is the subset of region-based advertising and marketing. Both those types of marketing target clients primarily based on the geographical positioning.

The difference basically lies inside the radius of targeting. Proximity advertising and marketing is an extra granular form of advertising. It may be as precise as 10 meters around a painting at a museum or, 50 meters round a newly launched vehicle in a dealership. Location-based advertising, however, is not always as correct and focused because the preceding form.

Which of the two is usually recommended to your business?

Depending on the use case you want to apply it for, you can select between proximity advertising and marketing and vicinity-based advertising. If the use-case is precise in nature and wants to address a smaller area, opt for proximity advertising. On the opposite hand, if use-case entails a bigger radius, as an example, some kilometres then choose region-based totally marketing.

What is the geo-concentrated on?
Geo-targeting is technically a subdomain of geo-fencing that objectives only people that fit unique standards. Geo-concentrated on determines the focused on standards using demographics, pastimes, and behaviours.

Unlike geo fencing that promotes a widespread provided to everyone within the centred radius, geo-concentrated on promotes to a crowd. For instance, promoting the loyalty programs most effective to those customers of your enterprise.

What is Geo-conquesting?
Geo-conquesting is a region-based advertising technology that focuses on attracting the customers of competitors toward your enterprise the use of location-based commercials.

These ads target the customers of your opponents and convince them that your products/offerings/offers are better than that of your competition.

What is geo quarter conversion reporting?

Geo Zone Conversion or location-primarily based conversion reporting is the method of the usage of location-primarily based services to gain conversions each on-line and offline.

For instance, the usage of beacon analytics in a retail keep to analyse footfall metrics, maximum visited and least visited sections, visitors at the billing counter and many others.

This evaluation can provide you with a clean perception of the difference among what number of people visited your store and how many people sold your merchandise. These records will be of notable use whilst you optimise your business.

How can you target the audience who have grown to become off location on their smartphones? Google clearly tracks area statistics from Android gadgets even though they have location offerings disabled.

Google declares that it is true for consumers to permit themselves to be tracked and it is widely recognized that the organisation keeps the consumer's private information relaxed. Users should manually change the settings on their telephone to prevent Google from sending them region-based pointers.

In what approaches are Bluetooth Beacons higher than GPS?

- Beacons do not require any net connectivity to acquire notifications.

- Beacons can track indoor movements however GPS cannot

- Beacons are quicker than GPS

- Beacons are more unique

7. Augmented reality

Consider environments where digital information and affects are used to support a product or service or environment. Augmented reality is the era that expands our physical reality, adding layers of digital records onto it. Unlike Virtual Reality (VR), AR does not create the whole artificial environments to update actual with a digital one. AR appears in direct view of a present surroundings and adds sounds, videos, pictures to it.

A view of the actual-world environment with superimposed laptop-generated photographs, therefore changing the perception of reality, is the AR (Realitytechnologies.com,2018).

The term itself was coined again in 1990, and one of the first industrial uses were in television and army. With the rise of the Internet and smartphones, AR rolled out its second wave and nowadays is broadly speaking associated with the interactive concept. Three-D models are directly projected onto bodily things or fused collectively in real-time, diverse augmented truth apps impact our habits, social life, and the leisure enterprise.

AR apps generally join virtual animation to a unique 'marker', or with the help of GPS in phones pinpoint the area. Augmentation is occurring in real time and inside the context of the environment, for example, protecting rankings to a stay feed recreation, activities.

There are four varieties of augmented fact today:

- marker less AR

- marker-primarily based AR

- projection-primarily based AR

- superimposition-based totally AR

Brief history of AR

AR within the Sixties. In 1968 Ivan Sutherland and Bob Sproull created a primary head-hooked up show, known as The Sword of Damocles. Obviously, it became a difficult tool that displayed primitive laptop pics.

AR within the Seventies. In 1975 Myron Krueger created Video place – an artificial reality laboratory. The scientist predicted the interplay with virtual items by means of human actions. This concept later changed into use for certain projectors, video cameras, and onscreen silhouettes.

AR within the 1980s. In 1980 Steve Mann evolved a first transportable computer known as Eye Tap, designed to be worn in the front of the eye. It recorded the scene to superimposed consequences on it later, and displays it all to a consumer who may also play with it via head movements. In 1987 Douglas George and Robert Morris evolved the prototype of a heads-up show (HUD). It displayed astronomical facts over the real sky.

AR inside the Nineteen Nineties. The year 1990 marked the beginning of the "augmented reality" time period. It first regarded in Thomas Caudell and David Mizell – Boeing agency researchers. In 1992 Louis Rosenberg of America Air Force created the AR device called "Virtual Fixtures". In 1999, a set of scientists led by way of Frank Delgado and Mike Abernathy examined new navigation software program, which generated runways and streets statistics from a helicopter video.

AR inside the 2000s. In 2000 a Japanese scientist Hirokazu Kato developed and published ARToolKit – an open-source SDK. Later it became adjusted to work with Adobe.

In 2004 Trimble Navigation presented an out of doors helmet-established AR gadget. In 2008 Wikitude made the AR Travel Guide for Android cell devices.

AR today. In 2013 Google beta tested the Google Glass – with internet connection thru Bluetooth. In 2015 Microsoft provided two modern technologies: Windows Holographic and HoloLens (an AR goggles with plenty of sensors to show HD holograms). In 2016 Niantic released Pokémon Go sport for cellular gadgets. The app blew the gaming industry up and earned $2 million in its first week.

How does Augmented Reality work?
What is Augmented Reality for many of us implies a technical facet, i.e. How does AR work? For AR a certain variety of data (images, animations, videos, three-D models) can be used and people will see the result in each natural and synthetic light.

Also, customers are privy to being inside the real world that is superior by way of computer vision, not like in VR.

AR may be displayed on various devices: monitors, glasses, hand-held devices, cell telephones, head-set up displays. It involves technology like S.L.A.M. (simultaneous localization and mapping), depth monitoring (in brief, a sensor data calculating the space to the items), and the following additives:

Cameras and sensors. Collecting facts approximate consumer's interactions and sending it for processing. Cameras on gadgets are scanning the environment and with this information, a tool locates bodily items and generates 3D styles. It can be special responsibility cameras, like in Microsoft HoloLens, or commonplace cell phone cameras to take pictures/videos. Processing.

AR devices in the end ought to act like little computer systems, something modern-day smartphones already do. In the identical manner, they require a CPU, a GPU, flash reminiscence, RAM, Bluetooth/Wi-Fi, a GPS, and so on.

To track speed, attitude, direction, orientation in area and so on.

Projection. This refers to a miniature projector on AR headsets, which takes facts from sensors and projects digital content material (result of processing) onto a surface to view. In fact, using projections in AR has now not been fully invented yet to apply it in business services or products.

Reflection. Some AR gadgets have mirrors to help human eyes to view virtual snap shots. Some have an "array of small curved mirrors" and some have a double-sided replicate to mirror linked to a Digi-cam and to a user's eye. The goal of such reflection paths is to carry out a right photograph alignment.

Types of Augmented Reality

Marker-based AR. Some also call it to picture recognition, because it calls for a special visual object and a Digi-cam to scan it. It can be anything, from a broadcast QR code to important signs. The AR device additionally calculates the location and orientation of a marker to put the content, in a few cases. Thus, a marker initiates digital animations for users to view, and so pix in a mag may additionally become 3-D fashions.

Marker less AR. A.K.A. Area-primarily based or position-based augmented reality, that makes use of a GPS, a compass, a gyroscope, and an accelerometer to offer statistics based on consumer's location. This data then determines what AR content material you locate or get in a certain region. With the provision of smartphones this kind of AR generally produces maps and instructions, nearby corporations info. Applications include activities and information, business advertisements pop-ups, navigation assist.

Projection-based AR. Projecting artificial light to physical surfaces, and in some cases allows one to engage with it. These are the holograms we have all seen in sci-fi movies like Star Wars. It detects consumer interaction with a projection via its alterations.

Superimposition-primarily based AR. Replaces the original view with an augmented, fully or in part. Object reputation performs a key role without it the whole idea is truly impossible.

We have all seen the example of superimposed augmented truth in IKEA Catalogue app, that lets in customers to vicinity virtual objects of their fixtures catalogue of their rooms.
Augmented reality gadgets

Many modern devices already help Augmented reality. From smartphones and tablets to devices like Google Glass or handheld devices, and those technology work to adapt. For processing and projection, AR devices and hardware to start with have requirements including sensors, cameras, accelerometer, gyroscope, digital compass, GPS, CPU, shows, and matters we've already referred to.

Devices suitable for Augmented reality fall into the subsequent classes:

Mobile gadgets (smartphones and tablets) – the maximum available and high-quality fit for AR cellular apps, starting from pure gaming and leisure to enterprise analytics, sports, and social networking.

Special AR gadgets, designed basically and entirely for augmented reality studies. One example is head-up displays (HUD), sending facts to show at once, into user's view.

Originally delivered to train military combatants pilots, now such devices have applications in aviation, car industry, production, sports activities, and many others.

AR glasses (or clever glasses) – Google Glasses, Meta 2 Glasses, Laster See-Thru, LA forge AR eyewear, and so forth. These devices are able to show notifications out of your phone, supporting meeting line workers, get right of entry to content material hands-unfastened, and so forth.

AR contact lenses (or clever lenses), taking Augmented Reality one step even farther. Manufacturers like Samsung and Sony have introduced the improvement of AR lenses. Respectively, Samsung is running on lenses because the accessory links to smartphones, while Sony is designing lenses as separate AR devices (with features like taking photos or storing data).

Virtual retinal shows (VRD), developing pics via projecting laser light into the human eye. Aiming at vivid, excessive assessment and excessive-resolution photographs, such systems but continue to be to be made for a practical use.

Possible applications of AR

Augmented reality might also supplement our everyday activities in various approaches. For instance, one of the most popular programs of AR is gaming. New AR games provide plenty better experiences to players, some even promote a more active outgoing manner of existence (Pokémon Go, Ingress).

Gaming grounds are being moved from virtual spheres to actual existence, and players perform certain activities.

 For instance, a simple health club pastime for children by using the Canadian agency SAGA, where to crack cubes on a wall kids hit it with a ball.

AR in retail may also act to deliver higher customer engagement and retention, as well as emblem cognizance and more sales. Some capabilities might also assist clients make wiser purchases – supplying product information with 3-D models of any length or shade. Real estate also can benefit from Augmented Reality thru 3D tours of apartments and homes, that can also be manipulated to amend a few elements.

Other capability areas for AR encompass:

- Education: interactive models for studying and training functions, from mathematics to chemistry.

- Medicine/healthcare: to assist diagnose, monitor, train, localize, etc.

- Military: for superior navigation, marking gadgets in actual time.

- Art / installations / visual arts / song.

- Tourism: data on destinations, sightseeing items, navigation, and instructions.

- Broadcasting: enhancing stay activities and event streaming by means of protecting content material.

- Industrial design: to visualize, calculate or version.

REVISION
- What is AR in MM, utilise 50 words to outline key elements

- If you owned a florist shop in 150 words explain how and why you would utilise MM geo fencing, to build footfall sales.

OBJECTIVES
MM best practices ensures that a MM campaign is on point to deliver and provide one's customers with a good experience whilst understanding good conduct and regulations.

Chapter Learning Outcomes
- To comprehend the practices of MM
- To understand MM applications in marketing today
- An appreciation of MM benefits in a marketing context

Critical thinking
Having completed this topic, one will be able to:
- Appreciate the development of MM practices and discuss it
- Have an appreciation of MM integration in marketing to date
- Be able to consider the infusion of MM

Critical thinking
Having completed this topic, one will be able to:
- Discuss and debate MM practices as a topic
- Analyse MM regulations and understand it
- Consider MM application in a work setting

The purpose of mobile marketing should be to relate to customers' needs and attract more business so mobile marketing should be integrated into the marketing program. Remember to ensure the website is mobile friendly and fully optimised, this is a key component in mobile marketing as stated around 70 per cent of individuals return to the website if the mobile contact is a good experience. In some studies, it was reported that some 61 per cent of users will leave the website if it does not link effectively on mobile, recall in the last year there was an 80 per cent increase in global mobile traffic with some 60 per cent of the global level traffic coming from smartphones.

The mobile web is growing some eight times faster than web adoption in the late 90s and more people are projecting to do more shopping on the mobile devices going forward. However, shoppers want a good experience on their mobile with around a third abandoning transactions due to poor performance. It is estimated around 40 plus per cent of Internet traffic will be mobile in 2018 and this will support increases in consumers having a higher opinion or brands that offer a good mobile experience.

People who enjoy using the mobile to make purchases are looking for a strong landing page that is maximised in terms of format and content, mobile marketing needs to be efficient to be effective.

There are many ways to complete mobile marketing, below are some reasoned examples:

Permission-based mobile marketing
There is a range of definitions in basic terms it is requesting consent from consumers to communicate on the mobile device. The principal reason for using permission-based mobile marketing is that commonly it leads to better engagement with consumers, better returns on investment and a much higher response rate. Is also recognised that it supports brands in the creation of lasting relationships and therefore lifetime equity, as mobile marketing supports brand values and propositions. It is a two-stage process first to get consent and then secondly positive database management.

Instead of the shotgun approach using bulk phone numbers, by gaining customer consent first, it allows the marketer to gain consumer confidence because the consumer has agreed and given permission through voice, email, website, text or phone message. Always make sure that customers can change their preferences and opt out of the permission granted.
Positive database management means the ability of the marketing team to slice and dice information on the customer base reflecting their interests, location, attitudes, demographic details and behaviour patterns, using a database management system. By adopting a consent based platform, companies can get to know the user and profile them whilst analysing the success of mobile marketing campaigns through the subscribers. Statistics support that over 50% of markers segment subscriber information based on the purchase history engagement behaviour.

Geo Fencing
This concert features of the use of GPS and also RFID to define and track geographic boundaries of an area, geo fencing creates a radius around a specific location for example the supermarket, Fashion store, School, public building. If you consider a helicopter view of a map of a suburban suburb with street names and buildings you can then location-based mark the area that will be targeted with predefined messages, ads and offers delivered to the user of the mobile.

By now, you have probably heard of geo fencing, or the organising of a virtual fence around a predefined geographic area. Maybe you have even sent a geofenced push notification yourself, however one continues to have a few questions about how the generation works and, extra importantly, how to make push notifications work for your business.

Let us hit the basics first. Say one decides to build an app on your small commercial enterprise with an internet app builder. Push notifications are one of the first-class available app functions with the most ability for return on investment—and geo fencing takes push notifications even further.

When considered one of your app customers enters or exits a geofenced place, a focused push notification is sent immediately to their tool. This timely, applicable cell messaging is outstanding for customer engagement. Users hear about offers or announcements after they're within the location and able to act on them.

Many agencies use geo fencing to really drive special offers to clients when they stroll or move close to an enterprise's region. But there's lots of opportunity for creativity. For example, actual property agencies can push notifications to viable consumers when they arrive close to open houses, and bands can ship messages to fans when they stroll by a concert venue the band may be performing at soon. But there's no real restriction on vicinity. Coffee shops may want to trigger geo fenced push notifications while customers are downtown and in want of a coffee.

A wedding planner ought to set up a geo fenced push notification around bridal stores and bakeries, providing helpful buying guidelines or highlighting the quality deals for customers. Retail shops should alert users to offers once they're close by the nearby mall. The opportunities are broad. If you're innovative, geo fencing can function an outstanding income and consumer retention device.

What is the correct size for a geo fenced region?

It is clear that organizations can set the radius of their predominant place's geo fence to anything size they want, however how big is too big? Well, a citywide radius is glaringly too big, it lacks the place-based relevance that makes geo fencing an amazing engagement tool.
 Instead, if your commercial enterprise has plenty of competition, it's nice to recognise your personal backyard. Try your neighbourhood first. If you are no longer producing the attention you want, make bigger a piece.

Now that we have answered the query of precisely "What is Geo fencing", let us consider other issues. It is not always about approximately bombarding customers with messages any place they pass. If you try this, they will decide out of your messaging altogether or, worse, uninstall your app. Instead, the consumer has to come back first. Always consider whether or not or no longer you will want to acquire your messages as a hypothetical consumer, and consider the value your program affords.

To accomplish this, do not think about geo fencing as just another other way to sell to your audience. Instead, use it as an organic manner to connect and add value. You would not want your favourite groups exploited by each channel to boost sales aggressively, however if they pop up once in a while with something timely, applicable, and beneficial, it may be of real interest.

Your intention ought to be to leverage geo fencing to improve your customers' reports and provide them with up sides. If you can do this, even as additionally driving site visitors for your location and pastime in your promotions, all the better.

Geo fencing has increased significantly as it has become recognised to have many benefits including enticing customers to a particular location, sending redeemable coupons that the location, enhancing customer loyalty through a powerful experience and increasing brand awareness.

Geo fencing for mobile marketing is now recognised is so strong strategy that improves engagement and builds customer relationships as it allows the customer to engage with the band other place in time it is convenient localised and relevant to that location of the customer.

 Looking at the literature on the interest customers have in mobile applications that deliver geo targeted coupons on the smartphone 50 per cent claims there were very interested, interested was somewhat interested in this technology.

Imagine being able to deliver a local promotion almost instantly using mobile that attracts interest from a range of customers that can be even time, based for example 20 per cent off if you buy Levi jeans between 1pm and 3pm today.

Further Discussion

Creating an app for your organisation
Research literature exposes that the total time spent in apps grew 60 per cent on android in one year, estimates claiming that global mobile app downloads will reach 284 billion by 2020.

Research also supports some 80 per cent odd per cent of consumers interviewed prefer mobile apps to mobile websites. Mobile apps allow the marketer to contact loyal customers 24/ 7.

Like such a lot of marketers earlier than you, you have got a fantastic app concept burring to your mind, and you don't have any idea a way to convey it and all of its profit potential to fruition. And like the ones who've paved the way for app entrepreneurs, you want to analyse the ropes.

While a few will suggest you to rent a developer and make investments a fortune on your idea, realists will tell you the hazard is just too huge.

 There are tons of app building applications accessible that assist you to make your vision a truth, however the easy reality is with some making plans and methodical paintings on your element, the system is reasonably simple.

Let's begin at the very beginning of the way to create an app, refer to material cited at (Biznessapps.com, 2018).

How to Build an App – Step 1: Set a Goal.

Step faraway from any shape of technology and get out a pen and paper and outline what it is you want to accomplish.
The beginning line within the app improvement word is a pen and paper, now not complex coding and designing. Ask and solution the following questions:

- What exactly do you need your app to do?

- How are you going to make it attraction to customers?

- What hassle is it going to resolve?

- How will it simplify lifestyles for people?

- How will you market your app?

- App building desires

Before you do something, create a clean picture of what you need carried out!

How To Build An App – Step 2: Sketch your Ideas.

Now you need to use a pen and paper that has the answers to the questions on your apps motive to broaden a sketch of what it will seem like. Here you circulate your worded ideas into visual representations of your mind.

Decide in case you are going to present your app to provide commercials to generate money, or are you going to offer it as a paid download. You also can choose the choice to offers in app purchases.

App idea constructing

How To Build An App – Step 3: Research, research, after which research a few extra.

Now you may turn your pc on, however do not start blindly designing your app. The leg work is nowhere near performed. You need to dig deep and study the options of your app idea. Realize that you have got one type of idea, but the numbers odds wise are someone else has already attempted it. You can observe this in two distinctive ways.

One you could become deflated and give up, or two, you may take a look at the competition and make your app stronger. Read the competition's reviews.

What did people like/dislike about the app? Then, use that information to your advantage. Refer back in your pen and paper from step one and, and adjust and adjust your concept.

After reading and modifying, your research desires, shift consciousness. It is time to harness the strength of the Internet. Is your app an honestly viable idea?

Here is wherein you may observe copyright restrictions and feasible technical holds ups. This step is essential because it will save you money ultimately. You cannot move ahead and spend time on a concept that will not work.

App constructing studies

Next, shift your research consciousness to income and advertising. Reflect again in your working, approximately how you will make cash with your app. Are you going to stay with your unique idea, or are you going to exchange it? What is your niche? Are you advertising and marketing to teenagers, parents, youngsters, instructors, travellers, gamers? Determine that focus on audience properly.

It will assist you narrow down design ideas.

After you have exhausted your foresight thinking, you could begin the fun creative stuff. Start to look for design ideas. 99design is an incredible exhibit for analysing new and revolutionary layout ideas. Browse via and notice what suits your goals. Keep your audience in thought when examining designs. A visual appeal is crucial.

How To Build An App – Step 4: Wireframe

In the era world, a wireframe is a glorified story board. Here is where you are taking your caricature and your layout idea, and also you deliver your idea a touch more readability and capability. This becomes the muse to your app's development, so it surely is an important step.

There are many wire framing websites that you can use to help you bring your sketches to virtual lifestyles with capability like click on through and icons.

The trick is locating one that you like and that is easy with a purpose to use.

Wire framing

Check out those wire framing tools here:

http://www.Axure.Com/
https://balsamiq.Com/merchandise/mockups/
http://pidoco.Com/
http://visio.Microsoft.Com/
http://www.Adobe.Com/products/indesign.Html?PID=7609893

http://iplotz.Com/
https://evernote.Com/penultimate/?Var=2
https://www.Omnigroup.Com/
https://www.Gliffy.Com/

How to Build an App – Step 5: Start Defining the Back End of Your App

We left off together to consider wireframe, so at this point for your app improvement, you have got a storyboard of the way you need your app to characterise.
Now it's time to apply that storyboard to begin examine capability. Using your wireframe, you need to delineate your servers, APIs, and data diagrams. There are a few first-rate do-it-yourself app builders that may provide you with the tools to easily do this.

Some of them even do if for you. If you are unclear of what this technical jargon approach, you have to probably use a service that offers web hosting and a method of amassing information approximately your app usage.

Regardless of what method you select to use to develop your app, it is vital that clear diagrams are created as they function the directions for everybody working on your task. Should you run across any technical difficulties, you need to revise your wireframe to mirror any adjustments.

Check out these lower back stop services:

https://www.Parse.Com/
http://www.Applicasa.Com/
http://www.Kinvey.Com/

How to Build an App – Step 6: Check Your Model

If you want to revise any of the layouts or navigation paths, do so. Keep your customers in thoughts, and try to comply with their questioning, not your own.

How To Build An App – Step 7: Get Building

With the inspiration in vicinity, you could start to place the puzzle together to constructing your app. First, your developer will set up your servers, databases, and APIs.

If you are using a do-it-yourself app builder, this could be finished for you. Do now not overlook to mirror at the comments you acquire from your testers. Modify the apps capability to mirror any adjustments you made based on your first section of checking out.

At this point, it's time to sign up for the app stores. You need to create an account with Google Play and Apple so you can get your app in the marketplace.
It may also take some days to undergo the method, so do not procrastinate this step.
Check out these app constructing platforms:

http://www.Biznessapps.Com
http://www.Kony.Com
https://appery.Io/
https://eachscape.Com

How To Build An App – Step 8: Design the Look

Now it is time to hire the designers to create your UI, person interface. The consumer interface is a vital part of your app due to the fact humans are drawn to how matters look and how clean they are to navigate. Through the design process, you need to preserve the remarks you obtain from your testers in thoughts, and you want to make sure the layout and the navigation reflect the comments you acquired.

If you've hired a graphic designer on your app, you may need to get excessive resolution, or visually appealing screens primarily based for your wireframe, for your app.

If you're using a WYSIWYG editor, you want to select your template and layout for your monitors yourself. Keep checking out consumer remarks in thoughts while growing the look of your app. You are constructing for users not for you!

App building designs

Check out these app design corporations:

http://www.Bluefountainmedia.Com/
http://bigdropinc.Com/
https://huemor.Rocks
http://www.Eight25media.Com/
http://www.Loungelizard.Com/
http://www.Inflexioninteractive.Com/

How To Build An App – Step 9: Test Your App, AGAIN.

A 2nd round of checking out is imperative. In this spherical, you will have each a functioning app as well as a person interface to test. All the screens of your app must well painted on this factor, and your app have to be visually appealing as nicely.

You want to run a battery of exams on your app in its finished form to guarantee that each the appearance and the feel of the app meet your expectancies. Proto.Io and Pixate are high-quality platforms for testing your app. Both of those packages will allow you to upload clickable links to navigate your app.

They will help you examine the very last layers, interactions, and design of your app as properly. You can use the statistics you get from this trying out segment that will help you move forward.

You may be scratching your head and asking, "Did I not do this with my wireframe?" The answer is, "well, sort of." While this will seem similar to your wireframe, it's lots more distinctive.
Your wireframe turned into just the skeleton of your app. At this factor, your app must be each aesthetically beautiful in addition to functioning.

How To Build An App – Step 10: Modify and Adjust

You have taken your prototype for a spin, and also you have learned that there are still some tweaks you need to make. Now that you have seen your app in its absolute functioning form, you want to call the backroom troops and ask them to do the identical.

Ask the equal individuals who regarded your app is it an improvement, examine it in it checking out section. Again, open yourself up to positive complaint, and use the remarks for this reason. Lastly, ask your developer and your designer to make any adjustments that you're feeling would be treasured to your app.

How To Build An App – Step 11: Beta Testing

You have looked at your app thru numerous special lenses, and you watched and managed to expand functioning, aesthetically eye-catching, hassle fixing app. Now, you need to look at how your app goes to function in a live environment.

Android makes this process simple iOS likes to maintain things in a managed surrounding. There is pros and cons to each procedure but the bottom line is you need to jump through one final hoop. You can clearly upload your app file on any android tool and test it in any surroundings.

IOS requires you to operate a platform called TestFlight to beta take a look at your app. Apple is quite thorough with its directions and instructions for the usage of its beta check platform.
A first-rate function to this beta testing choice is that you can invite testers to check your app earlier. It is put some other person lens through which to view your app.

App testing build

You have made it to the finish line. You have brought your concept to fruition, and the remaining step is to percentage it with the competitive arena.

Hopefully, you have long gone on to resolve any prime troubles. If not, with a bit of luck your app has a few functions that can simplify or bring amusement to someone's lifestyles. Regardless, you've performed something big. Now it's time to distribute it!

Android and iOS, once more are very one of a kind with reference to advertising apps. If you stay with this commercial enterprise, you'll see a sample emerge—Android is a touch less strict.
 Again, there are pros and cons to each approaches, but as an app entrepreneur, you will need to research the rules for both.

You can truly upload your app to the android shop. It will now not be reviewed right away. You will instantly be selling your app inside the Google Play keep. IOS, on the other hand, will overview your app earlier than it could cross stay. While there is no set time body for the Apple team to review your app and push it at the shelves, you may guestimate approximately every week of ready.

App shop

If you are disturbing about getting your app onto the devices of users, you may additionally submit it in Pre-Apps. This is a notable opportunity to have your app regarded by using folks that like to have a first examine new thoughts.

Keep in thought, these consumers are always reviewing up and coming thoughts, so their comments can be remarkable for you. They are familiar with #trending apps, so one would advise taking this extra step—if for not anything more than to learn extra approximately the app global benefits.

One needs to remember that you still must promote your app. Just because your app is in place does no longer suggest you are going to begin making millions tomorrow. Sadly, advertising cannot simply be brought onto this guide as "Step thirteen".

It's got quite a few steps of its own. So, now that one realizes a way to make an app, it is suggested one to start getting to know app advertising strategies so you can change the world one app at a time!

Update subscriber data
In mobile marketing it is important to understand that the information you hold on consumers will grow stale and inaccurate overtime as people change locations, mobile numbers. To be effective updating subscriber data ensures information held on the database is clean an up-to-date.

One way of keeping databases clean is to send a simple text message to a subscriber asking them for the latest information on current location, types of offers they are interested in. Consumers find it beneficial receiving relevant and personalised offers on their mobile at home or on the move.

There is nothing worse the receiving information that lacks relevance it ends up in the bin.

Mobile Ad Extensions
Many search engines allow ad extensions, the provides additional information about your business with the ad exposed. Imagine an ad on Google for a fashion retail store next to the ad is an extension of a telephone with a call now message to receive a benefit such as a free offer, 10% off, buy one get one free.

Extensions make your ad standout when consumers are searching on their mobile using mobile ad extensions that are automated or in fact manual, the automated extensions are added by Google electronically, the manual ad extensions are the ones the marketing team controls.

The benefits of these types of mobile ad extensions and specifically those are manually is that the marketer can include items such as my ball at extensions, offer extensions, click to call extensions, site link extension and location extension.

A mobile app extension is like the click to call extension you can send people to the download page of your app on the mobile device. One can link an app with the extension giving marketers a new distribution channel. Offer extensions allow advertisers to attach an offer for example 10% off below the displayed ad and as a consumer uses clickable link to redeem the coupon or instant discount. Linked with local extensions it can be an effective way of driving sales.

Site links extension
This mobile ad extension allows for multiple pages of your site, customers just have to click on the relevant pages on your site. Multiple site links to the ad using for example Google ad words shows site links randomly with the best performing site links replacing poor performers.

It is a tidy way of emphasising messages to extend headline, use call our extensions, provides site links such as deals and special offers, most popular, tomorrow's events, stock is running out.

Location Extension
Most people using mobiles look for information on the location of where products and services can be purchased from physical environments such as wholesalers and retailers. By placing the location address in a mobile ad, it increases the visibility of the ad and makes it easier for the reader to find where to go.

Some four in ten consumers still purchase items from retail establishments for many reasons. Some expensive items need to be seen before purchase such is cars, white goods. Research indicates the sellers of goods and services who have a bricks and mortar outlets find location extension on mobile devices increase traffic and sales.

REVISION
- In 200 words as the owner of a local flower shop outline why an app would benefit the business. What steps would you use to develop the app.

MOBILE TOOLS -8

OBJECTIVES
There are a collection of mobile tools available to choose from either one or a collection, each act differently thus choice needs to be made based on knowledge of the market and target customer.

Chapter Learning Outcomes
- To comprehend the tools of MM
- To understand MM applications pluses and minuses in marketing today
- An appreciation of MM blending in a marketing context

Critical thinking
Having completed this topic, one will be able to:
- Appreciate the development of MM platforms and discuss them
- Have an appreciation of MM platform capability in marketing to date
- Be able to consider the benefits of each MM tool

Critical thinking
Having completed this topic, one will be able to:
- Discuss and debate MM tools as a topic
- Analyse MM tool material and understand it
- Consider MM application in a work setting

To assist marketers to build, conduct and control mobile marketing there are some handy tools available which make this job much easier. Here some, using explanations from company web sites.

1. Flurry
This is a platform that acts nearly like a representative for each of your cellular advertising campaigns. You can use it that will help you customize your campaigns to help make sure that your goals are met whenever. Flurry works to assist optimize cell experience of customers through better apps and private ads.
Flurry is a high-quality device for groups trying to begin on their cellular campaign and attain customers on their smartphones and capsules.

2. Slick Text
This tool offers one of the simplest approaches to create an SMS advertising listing and to ship out texts on your consumers or subscribers.

You reserve a keyword and have fascinated users' text that keyword to 31996. Everybody who does that is routinely added in your list.

After that, any time you want to compose or send a text in your listing, you log in, compose your message, and send it.

3. AppNext

You can use this tool to monetize your mobile efforts even similarly via promoting the cell apps which are most relevant on your users. Essentially, you perceive and propose the apps on your customers, and you receive charge with each download.

Sometimes, these quick and easy approaches of creating a chunk more revenue are simply what are needed while it is time to create increases.

4. Kiip

Use Kiip to construct customer loyalty and create business increase via creating the ideal rewards program on your target market.
For instance, if you are a fitness company, you may reward consumers with a downloadable replica of an intensive health video after they have logged forty hours of workout for your internet site.

The app refers to this as finding moments that you could celebrate together with your customers.

5. RevMob

If you have apps or cell websites, you could use RevMob to put the right advertising on ones web sites. If you are an advertiser, RevMob will help you to target the right consumers to your cellular advertising campaigns.

They also provide many creative advertising options including banner commercials, video, and rich media.
This answer is likewise cellular platform agnostic, which means that it is miles stronger for Amazon, Android, and iPhone users.

6. DeCarta

Local is extra critical than ever. In truth, it's so essential that Uber has lately obtained DeCarta. It will be exciting to look what occurs in the destiny.
This tool gives you the capacity to provide your customers with neighbourhood search skills, and the capacity to decide what locations of hobby are near them.

7. PlaceIQ

Imagine how useful it would be to understand the behaviours, interests, conduct, and reviews of people inside a given locale. This is what PlaceIQ does for you.

It provides you with insights, based totally upon amassed information that you can then use to personalize your cell advertising efforts based upon the area that you are focused on.

The greater place-primarily based intelligence that you have, the extra focused and more powerful your cell efforts are going to be.

8. TXT180

This is a completely simple, inexpensive, however fairly viable SMS texting answer. If you're inquisitive about auto reaction, sending out scheduled messages, the use of textual content in contests to create rewards programs, or for creating text for more info campaigns, this might be an exquisite solution for your company.

9. AppoDeal

Imagine if you simplest had to attention on development and advertising and that the monetization aspect became looked after for you. If you make use of AppoDeal, this is exactly what happens. It works by means of monitoring person interest and conduct, and then locating the first-class and maximum moneymaking classified ads to show to your behalf.

10. WebTrends

This is a no brainer. Simply find out how purchasers are interacting with your logo throughout an expansion of channels. Then, you can use the insights supplied to you to sharpen your mobile advertising efforts.

Even in case you are the use of Google Analytics or every other comparable bundle, you should keep in mind the extra valuable insights that you'll acquire.

11. ShopPad

This creates a simple, but fashionable cell platform that your visitors can use even as shopping on your cellular web site. It has a simple interface and a swish design that will assist to make sure that your clients stay engaged so long as you need them to.

12. MoPub

MoPub gives you the capability to manipulate your cellular advertising and marketing campaigns. Its functions consist of budgeting, evaluation, and even reporting that you can use to make certain that your campaigns run easily and that you can analyse from any gaps that arise.

You may not have heard of them yet, however Progressive Web Apps (PWA) are about to change the cell panorama. While introduced in 2015 with the aid of Google, PWAs have received recognition this 12 months. So earlier than it will become all of the rage, what are Progressive Web Apps precisely?

What is a PWA?

In the maximum simple sense, PWAs are mobile apps brought thru the net. This era permits PWAs to deliver an app-like enjoyment on your browser. It feels like a local app because of the use of an app-shell that offers app-style navigations and gestures. Since revolutionary apps are constructed on the net, they are no longer tied to specific gadgets. A PWA displays seamlessly and identically on all devices, which includes desktop, mobile, tablet, or anything comes subsequent.

iOS-android

What is extra, it allows a Progressive Web App to load instantly, no matter community being first-class. In different words, this net app is designed to visuals offline and in areas of low connectivity. With the help of pre-caching, it remains updated, serving the person with the most up-to-date content material upon launch. Similar to an app, the person is able to store the PWA to their domestic display screen to access it at any time. Making it installable, without the hassle of downloading it from the app stores.

PWA vs.Native Mobile App

While local cellular apps offer the highest fine user experience, they arrive with difficulty for each the consumer and the developer. One of the largest differences among PWAs and local apps is the presence of the "app keep intermediary".

For Progressive Web Apps, this middleman is completely taken out. For app developers, no app store method you are no longer restrained by means of iOS and Android's guidelines and pointers.
A developer will not go through an approval system, permitting the app for use as quickly as it is ready. There is also no want to manually replace the app, because the revised app version will immediately and routinely be to be had to anybody.

From the attitude of the end user, they may be able to get right of entry to the PWA while not having to download it from an app save.
Instead, a PWA is linkable, this means that all of us can release the app straight from a URL. You can share it on social media, electronic mail, textual content message, on-line ad, or hyperlink it to a QR code, and the person will instantly be immersed into an app.

By casting off all this friction, it will be less difficult for users to have access to the app. Consumers discover it tedious having to discover the app within the app store, watch for it to download, and fear that it'll use up all their storage space earlier than they could begin the use of the app. Because PWAs notably lessen the amount, of steps they need to take (basically making it a one-step process), there is a far higher risk of people certainly using the app. In fact, we use 4x as many websites as mobile apps, resulting in a much large ability user base with a web primarily based app.

Pwa-drift

Another predominant difference for app developers is that they will now not ought to adapt their app to iOS or Android. The fact that PWAs use net technology method they work cross-platform, on most browsers, taking the operating machine out of the equation.

You can construct one Progressive Web App and it will look and perform the equal across all gadgets. Users may have a cohesive revel in on any tool they pick to launch the app on.

Finally, PWAs are noticeably discoverable. This approach they are without difficulty identified by way of search engines like Google and yahoo, allowing them to arise in the search consequences much like another internet content material. PWAs will be dealt with traditional SEO, so it receives listed for more than simply the app name, but also the content inside the app. It will not be handled as an app in particular, however as a chunk of content material that could "solution" someone's "question."

To put this into context, 60 per cent of searches at the moment are from cell devices and this wide variety continues to grow. People are actively the use of their cell gadgets to find content, so imagine your PWA coming up in those search results. For example, a person might be looking for a salon inside the location, so that they use the Google search bar to start their inquiry.

The seek effects will maximum probable display directories like Yelp and salon web sites. If you very own a salon business, your PWA should rank in these searches, driving customers straight from the search effects on your app.

This first contact is an opportunity to transform your customers.
 An app-like revel in will allow customers to timetable a salon appointment from a UI built for cell.
It's a continuing system beginning with a web search and finishing with a completed undertaking within the app.

PWA vs. Mobile Website

PWAs are a hybrid of native apps and mobile websites, however how do they vary from responsive web sites? Unlike "vintage college" cellular web sites, PWAs are speedy. Note that fifty-three per cent of users will abandon a website if it takes longer than three seconds to load. PWAs load immediately, regardless of community, and offer rapid-to-respond interfaces. This removes their dependence at the network, as mobile websites do, making sure it is immediate and reliable for users. A PWA additionally updates inside the historical past, so customers never need to wait for new content material to load.

In addition, traditional cellular web sites consciousness on static statistics, at the same time as PWAs are able to provide users with dynamic functionality. PWAs offer an immersive full-display screen experience, permitting customers to location cellular meals orders, take part in a loyalty software and contact a commercial enterprise. It can also re-have interaction users with web push notifications, much like local push notifications.

Who Is Already Seeing Success?

Lancôme paw

To drive each traffic and re-engagement, cosmetics logo Lancôme launched a Progressive Web App to supply a quick, app-like revel into their clients.

Lancôme saw mobile visitors exceed desktop visitors for the first time in 2016. Despite a developing range of cellular website online visitors, cellular conversion fees didn't in shape those for laptop. 38 per cent of buying carts on computing device caused orders, at the same time as the conversion price for the mobile web changed into handiest 15 per cent.

These numbers found out that clients were experiencing large obstacles while seeking to purchase thru their cellular tool.

At first, Lancôme taken into consideration an e-commerce app as the answer. However, they understood that an app best made experience for clients who visited frequently. Mobile shoppers could now not go back to an e-trade app weekly, let alone each day, in order that they wouldn't see the cost in downloading a Lancôme app.

 The agency desired to build the proper person revel in on all of their gadgets. According to Google, "The business enterprise wished a fast-loading, compelling e-cellular enjoy, similar to what they could reap with a native app— however one that become also discoverable and on hand to everybody via the cellular net". Enter the Progressive Web App.

The outcomes was effective:

- 84% decrease in time until the page is interactive

- 17% increase in conversions

- 53% boom in cellular classes on iOS

- 18% open price on push notifications

- 8% of purchasers who faucet on a push notification make a buy

All advised, the PWA has been a wonderful fulfilment, assisting the beauty giant make incredible strides into the cell revolution.

What does the destiny appear to be?

While native cell apps are in no way going extinct, a PWA can provide an appropriate answer for businesses looking to construct a compelling and easily adoptable cellular place for their customers. PWAs provide the finest of both worlds, with all the share ability of the internet and all the capability of the local app.

It subsequently gives one the ability to enforce local functions into our web apps. One can be a part of the future of apps, wherein the mobile app and the cellular internet site emerge as one.

REVISION
- Using 150 words discuss in detail four mobile tools.

- Explain in 50 words ' what is PWA'.

- Research and find a successful mobile tool case study, outline it, in

  your own 100 words, discuss what were the 'objectives and strategies'

  adopted

SUMMARY -9

OBJECTIVES
Literature frameworks that (AI) has been around in some shape or form for many centuries, and in its basic form enabled the automation of tasks and thinking of using machines.

Chapter Learning Outcomes
- To comprehend the history of AI
- To understand AI applications in marketing today
- An appreciation of AI future in a marketing context

Critical thinking
Having completed this topic, one will be able to:
- Appreciate the development of AI and discuss it
- Have an appreciation of AI in marketing to date
- Be able to consider the future of AI

Critical thinking
Having completed this topic, one will be able to:
- Discuss and debate AI as a topic
- Analyse AI material and understand it
- Consider AI application in a work setting

Here are some short insights into what the destiny may additionally maintain for mobile marketers and entrepreneurs.

More effective concentration on consumers

In the previous couple of years, we have visible a real surge in concentration on customers thru cellular. Be it place primarily based, device precise or proximity marketing – the greater of your information that manufacturers and entrepreneurs can gather, the extra accurate (and therefore effective) the advertisements & mobile gives you'll acquire will be.

Presently, marketers are putting massive value on programmatic cellular advertising and marketing (additionally referred to as programmatic media shopping for) which is basically the usage of generation (along with an artificial intelligence system) if you want to automate the facilitation of buying and promoting advertisements to target a hyper-acute target market.

Have you ever looked for something on Google, just to see the exact element you have been simply searching at for five minutes in the past in your Facebook newsfeed?
This is programmatic advertising and marketing at work, though there's a whole lot of automation occurring behind the curtain.

Greater-powerful-targetting-of-purchasers-for-destiny-of-mobile-advertising, the future buying eco system will see advertising investment from advertisers and advertising agencies using ad servers they provide data tools such as social data, supplier data, DMP, exchanges. These will be linked to add server the supports Real time bidding and buying solutions.

The demand will come from brand, trade desks, DSPS and networks. The supply will come from SSP and ad networks. The audience will respond to the publisher using affiliate networks, sales houses and ad networks. Metrics will we used to understand the audience, Game web analytics, and complete post evaluation and effectiveness of campaigns.

While a few can also keep in mind this an invasion of private-ness, it is far commonplace among excessive profile targeted manufacturers and has been operating (often without the clients' expertise) for quite a few years now.

Suffice to say, it is one of the most effective and specific styles of acquiring targeted cell clients.

So how are we able to believe what programmatic advertising may additionally seem like in the near future? For example, synthetic intelligence systems are still in their infancy and feature a while to go before they will be capable of superior cognition of the human decision-making procedure. However, with huge strides inside the area of AI and development increasing at an exponential speed, we could be looking at a machine which could make choices as successfully (if now not greater so) than the average human.

Programmatic advertising is likely to come to be available to a wider target market at decreased prices. It is additionally possibly we will see advert companies adopting their personal programmatic assistants, programmable and capable of purchasing hundreds of ads every second – removing the want for human action.

Increased use of wearable tech

Wearables have emerged as all of the rage in current years, with Fitbit wristbands to track workout routines, and smart watches you may use to pay for your lunch – the adoption of wearable era has reached awesome proportions and recognition does no longer look in all likelihood to scale back anytime quickly. Needless to say, all this wearable tech comes with quite a few information items, and one can guess behind the scene that brands are getting more adept at logging, analysing and decoding this information as a good way to gain higher marketplace for their services and products.

Current trends aside, what can we expect from the future of wearables and the advertising strategies that stem from this industry? One can start studying these days patented wearables which are nevertheless in the same idea tiers.

For example, Japanese tech giants Sony have these days filed a patent for a smart touch lens that can report and store video with the blink of an eye.

It is safe to say that generation like this could alternate the game (again) for entrepreneurs and advertisers. Some have even taken into consideration an included digital assistant built into the eyepiece! Improvements-concentrated on-of-wearable-tech-for-destiny-of-mobile-advertising and marketing

The projected customer adoption of wearable tech by 2020 will hit $22.9 billion with compound growth of some 50 per cent from now to 2020. The Apple watch has made a big impact selling around 20 million units in 2018.Smart bands, watches, eye wear, transform-ables and others will drive the market for mobile. One can speculate that it is not too huge of a soar from interactive contact lenses to a cloud linked lens presenting centred advertising straight into the person's eye. Although this type of integration is likely to be way off, it is miles more likely to emerge as a possible invention.

Virtual and augmented reality advertising

The idea of virtual reality (VR) has been round for a while, with a lot of controversy over when the concept became first realized. Nonetheless, real technological know-how is slowly catching up with the imaginations of technology fiction and low and behold; VR and AR technologies are now turning into not unusual in purchase in society.
With entrepreneurs realizing the recognition of client VR and AR devices, and the immersive revelling in they provide, various virtual reality advertising companies together with Reverge have sprung up to fill this extremely sparkling area of interest. This is as well as mega-brands Coca Cola and McDonalds developing their personal VR campaigns, which just goes to expose there may be a growing call for those forms of professional advertising offerings.

Marketers have also been working up novel ways of use for VR technology including actual property sellers presenting digital residence excursions, VR rollercoasters featuring deep space battles, and greater immersion in on line gaming.

Back in 2014, Topshop and John Lewis were already experimenting with VR in their advertising, with Topshop imparting competition winners' virtual seats to the London style display and John Lewis debuting an interactive story presenting a small boy and his penguin.

So, with high street manufacturers finding their fit with virtual reality, and Facebook founder Mark Zuckerberg making an investment upwards of $2 Billion on the purchase of the Oculus VR, you could consider one is probably going to enjoy an increase in low cost VR era. But what can we count on from advertising and advertising inside the near future?

With digital reality reaching its penultimate goal of supplying a completely immersive environment, we are able to expect it will soon grow to be integrated with traditional kinds of marketing.

Imagine an immersive movie trailer with the viewer being able to experience the 2-minute clip in 360 degrees, with haptic feedback processors presenting contact and vibration to provide the consumer the feeling of being in the film.

The deployment of bots replacing human interaction

You might also already be aware of bots. For example, you could have seen the likes of Murphy Bot – which solutions your what-if question in the form of a photograph. Or prediction bots – supplying high-accuracy sports activities predictions. Or one can have already spoken to a bot unaware that it was not a human, inside the form of a chat bot on an ecommerce website.

For those who are not virtually positive what a bot is, it's a series of algorithms forming a software that can be programmed to perform automatic duties which include searching the net or performing moves on request.

The-deployment-of-bots-changing-human-interplay-for-future-of-mobile-advertising. The artistic expertise of Project Murphy is fantastic however it's nevertheless early days for bots.

With the likes of Apple's Siri & Microsoft's Cortana are getting increasingly more complicated and powerful as they are developed and refined, this is giving upward push to included bots imparting customer service and other such responsibilities formerly delegated to humans.

Though still in their infancy, bots at the moment are extra wise than ever before and people even have a tough time discerning whether they're talking to a real person or only a quite clever robotic. Needless to say, they are becoming pretty quintessential to personal experience.

So, with these conversational user interfaces being deployed in complete swing, what precisely are we able to expect from the future of internet bots? Aside from a Skynet-style robotic takeover of Earth, we are able to likely imagine artificially smart, system mastering running systems (sure, like inside the film Her) integrated right into a desktop laptop or mobile.

Since those systems develop as they examine, and are related to the internet 24/7, they could doubtlessly be able to permit you to know when the items you need are on sale, remind you of the events you are planning to attend, or order pizza for you without you having to even lift a finger.

The advertising advantages for this sort of generation are significant, and with automation becoming an element of the prevailing future.

The proliferation of AI in automated selection making

There had been many advances inside the field of AI in current years, with functions for your lifestyles you would not even recognize are governed via artificial intelligence algorithms.

The autocorrect function on your phone for example traces the patterns of your spelling, learns out of your previous mistakes and refines its prediction technique based totally on consumer enter mixed with a nifty machine mastering algorithm.

"The-proliferation-of-ai-in-computerized-decision-making-for-future-of-cellular-advertising is genuine and mobile marketers need to understand the software algorithms that are part of mobile marketing as they are the foundation architecture of mobile marketing," Seligman (2018).

1. Rule based decision making
Examples such as phone notification, time or threshold based alarms, simple pattern matching.
2. Statistical reasoning
Examples such as simple regression, numerical data, curve fitting, interpretation, outlier detection, predictive and maintenance
3. Machine Learning
Examples such as classification tasks, arbitrary data, features from large data sets, and quality control, using key metrics.
4. Artificial Intelligence
Examples such as dynamic adaption, automated selection, autonomous vehicles, human like conversation, intelligent digital assistant.

AI is another technological know-how coming to existence, yet how is it presently being included into nowadays mobile marketing and advertising efforts?

Google has made extremely progressive advances in gadget mastering and cognitive processing that has been effectively introducing these capabilities into their services and products for a while now, with AI generic in indexing web sites, opposite image search and YouTube guidelines.

It has even been incorporated into their ad network. IBM are also experiencing success with their flagship AI – Watson, who lately composed a track. Like Google, IBM have given the general public admission to the Watson Developer Cloud (their API) which means builders can now begin to produce apps and services for a selection of marketing functions – all offering AI. With all this new technology, the future is incredibly shiny for marketers and advertisers seeking to take their mobile campaigns to the following level, even though with matters turning into increasingly more complicated, it looks as if a steep learning curve in marketing theory and practice will be required.

Abduljalil, S., and Huam H.T., 2011. Attracting Consumers by Finding out Their Psychographic Traits. Malaysia: University Technology Malaysia.

Ahonen, T., 2010. The insider's guide to Mobile: The customers, Services, Apps, Phones, and Business of the Newest Trillion Dollar Industry. Hong Kong: Tomi Ahonen Consulting.

Ahonen, T., 2013. Mobile and Megatrends. In: Bruck, P. and Rao, M. (eds). Global mobile: applications and innovations for the worldwide mobile ecosystem. Medford: Information Today Inc.

Albright, C., (2017) Your six new ways to use Location Targeting, accessed 3 February 2018.

American Marketing Association, 2012. Marketing power - Dictionary. [online] Available at http://www.marketingpower.com/_layouts/Dictionary.aspx?dLetter=B (Accessed 2 February 2018).

Annalect (2017) Mobile Trends, Annalect.com, accessed 3 February,2018

Apostu, A., 2012. Perspectives on Big Data and Big Data Analytics. Available at: <http://dbjournal.ro/archive/10/10_1.pdf> [Accessed 5 February 2018].

Assuncao, M.D., 2014. Big Data computing and clouds: Trends and future directions. Elsevier. Available at: <http://dx.doi.org/10.1016/j.jpdc.2014.08.003>

Bagal, R., 2012. Multi-channel retailing – an introduction. [pdf] Available at: <http://www.microsretail.com/assets/category_files/pdf/RetailCustomerExperi ence_MultiChannelRetailing_Whitepa per.pdf> [Accessed 11 February 2018].

Balasubramanian S., Peterson R.,A., & Jarvenpaa S.,L., (2002) Exploring the Implications of M- Commerce for Markets and Marketing. Journal of Academy of Marketing Science 30(4): 348–361.

Barwise P & Farley JU (2005) The state of interactive marketing in seven countries: Interactive marketing comes of age. Journal of Interactive marketing 19(3): 67–80.

Baskin, J., 2012. The Semantics of Branding. Baskin Brand [blog] 23 April. Available at: http://baskinbrand.com/?p=485 [Accessed 14.05.2012].

Bauer, H., Reichardt, T., Barnes S, J., & Neumann, M., 2005. Driving consumer acceptance of mobile marketing: A theoretical framework and empirical study, Journal of Electronic Commerce, Research Six

Beaux., M., (2018) Mobile Apps are Dominating Display Advertising, Insights.marinsoftware.com, accessed 03 February, 2018.

Bezjian-Avery A., Calder B., & Iacobucci D., (1998) New Media Interactive Advertising Vs. Traditional Advertising. Journal of Advertising Research 38(4): 23–32.

Biznessapps.com, 2018 App maker and Mobile Apps for small Businesses, accessed 3 February 2018

Bonsor, K. 2010. How Augmented Reality Works. Retrieved March 30, 2018, from http://howstuffworks.com/ augmented-reality.htm

Brown, S.A., 2000. Customer Relationship Management - A Strategic Imperative in the World of e- Business. Ontario: John Wiley & Sons Canada Ltd.

Campbell, A., 2008. The power of branding. Canadian Underwriter, 75(10), pp. 16-20.

Caywood C.,L., Schultz D.,E., & Wang P., (1991) A Survey of Consumer Goods Manufactures. New York, NY: American Association of Advertising Agencies.

Connor, C. 2013, Who Wastes Time at Work, Forbes.com, Retrieved March 30, 2018.

Cuno, A., Z., 2005, Marketers get serious about the third screen, Advertising Age, July 11.

Dholakia R.,R., & Dholakia N., (2004) Mobility and Markets: Emerging Outlines of M- commerce. Journal of Business Research 57(12): 1391–1396.

Dhotre, M., 2010. Channel Management and Retail Marketing. Girgaon: Himalaya Publishing House.

Duncan T.,R., & Mulhern F., (eds) (2004) A White Paper on the Status, Scope and Future of IMC (from IMC Symposium sponsored by the IMC programs at Northwestern University and the University of Denver). New York, NY: McGraw-Hill.

Durkin M., & Lawlor M.,A., (2001) The Implications of the Internet on the Advertising Agency-Client Relationship. The Service Industries Journal 22(2): 175–190.

Ericsson AB, 2014. 10 Hot Consumer Trends 2015. [pdf] Available at: <www.ericsson.com/consumerlab> [Accessed 3 February 2018].

Ericsson AB, 2014. Ericsson mobility report [pdf] Ericsson AB. Available at: <http://hugin.info/1061/R/1872291/659558.pdf> [Accessed 3 February 2018].

Eslinger, T., 2014. Mobile Magic : The Saatchi and Saatchi Guide to Mobile Marketing and Design. Hoboken: Wiley.

Fahy, J. and Jobber, D., 2012. Foundations of Marketing. 4th ed. Berkshire: McGraw-Hill Education.

Ferrell, O.C., Hartline, M., 2014. Marketing Strategy. 6th ed. USA: South Western.

Flurry Analytics, State of Mobile 2015, Yahoo.com, accessed, 3 February 2018

Fournier, S., 1998. Consumers and Their Brands: Developing Relationship Theory in Consumer Research. Journal of Consumer Research, 24(4), pp. 343-353.

FOX News Network, LLC., 2013. The first mobile phone call was placed 40 years ago today. Available at: <http://www.foxnews.com/tech/2013/04/03/first-mobile-phone-call-was-placed-40- years-ago-today/> [Accessed 3 February 2018].

Friess, P. and Vermasan, O., 2013. Internet of Things: Converging Technologies for Smart Environments and Integrated Ecosystems. Aalborg: River Publishers.

Gambhir, A., 2013. Mobile Innovation Trends: Beyond the Hype Cycles. In: Bruck, P. and Rao, M. (eds). Global Mobile: Applications and Innovations for the Worldwide mobile ecosystem. Medford: Information Today Inc.

Gartner, 2014. Available at: Gartner's 2014 Hype Cycle for Emerging Technologies Maps the Journey to Digital Business. <http://www.gartner.com/newsroom/id/2819918> [Accessed 10 February 2018].

Harun, A., Kassim, A., Igau, O., Tahajuddin, S. and Al-Swidi, A., 2010. Managing Local Brands in Facing Challenges of Globalization: Be a Local or Global Leader? European Journal of Social Sciences, 17(2), pp. 254-265.

Heisterberg, R. and Verma, A., 2014. Creating Business Agility: How convergence of cloud, social, mobile, video and big data enables competitive advantage. Hoboken: Wiley.

Hougaard, S., and Bjerre, M., 2003. Strategic Relationship Marketing. Denmark: Samfunds literature Press.

Huang, R., Y., and Symonds, J., A., (2009) Mobile Marketing Evolution: Systematic Literature Review on Multi-Channel Communication and Multi-Characteristics Campaign, Enterprise Distributed Object Computing Conference Workshops, 2009. EDOCW 2009. 13th

Kapferer, J-N., 2008. The New Strategic Brand Management: creating and sustaining brand equity long term. 4th ed. London: Kogan Page.

Kaplan, A. M., 2011. If you love something, let it go mobile: Mobile marketing and mobile social media 4x4. Business Horizons, In Press, pp. 1-11.

Kaplan, A., 2014 Mobile Marketing Definition, Mashable.com. Accessed, 4 February, 2018

Karjaluoto, H., Leppäniemil, M., 2005 Factors influencing consumers' willingness to accept mobile advertising: A conceptual model, International Journal of Mobile Communications 3(3):197-213

Kitchen P.,J., & Schultz D.,E., (1999) A Multi-Country Comparison of the Drive for IMC. Journal of Advertising Research 39(1): 21–38.

Kitchen P.,J., Brignell J., Li T., & Spickett-Jones G., (2004) The Emergence of IMC: A theoretical Perspective. Journal of Advertising Research 44(March): 19–30.

Kliatchko J., (2005) Towards a New Definition of Integrated Marketing Communications (IMC). International Journal of Advertising 24(1): 7–34.

Kotler P., Wong V., Saunders J., & Armstrong G., (2005) Principles of Marketing (4th European edition). Essex: Pearson Education Limited.

Krum, C., 2012. Mobile Marketing: Finding Your Customers No Matter Where

Kurkovsky S., & Harihar K., (2006) Using ubiquitous computing in interactive mobile marketing. Personal and Ubiquitous Computing 10(4): 227–240.

Leppäniemil, M., Karjaluouto, H., 2008. Exploring the effects of gender, age, income and employment status on consumer response to mobile advertising campaigns, Journal of Systems and Information Technology, Vol. 10 Issue: 3, pp.251-265,

McMillan S.,J., & Hwang J.,S., (2002) Measures of Perceived Interactivity: An Exploration of the Role of Direction of Communication, User Control, and Time in Shaping Perceptions of Interactivity. Journal of Advertising 3(3): 41–54.

Melin, F. and Hamrefors, S., 2007. The Value-Creating Brand Strategy. Swedish Public Relations Association (Sveriges Informationsförening).

mma.global.com, (2018) v97 Introduction to mobile coupons, accessed 8 February 2018.

Mobile Marketing Association, Inc., 2009. MMA Updates Definition of Mobile Marketing. Available at: <http://mmaglobal.com/news/mma-updates-definition-mobile-marketing> [Accessed 4 February 2018].

Mobile Marketing Association, Inc., 2011. Mobile Advertising Guidelines. [pdf] Available at: <http://www.mmaglobal.com/files/mobileadvertising.pdf> [Accessed 8 February 2018].

Morgan, R.M. and Hunt, S.D., 1994. The Commitment-Trust Theory of Relationship Marketing. Journal of Marketing, 58(3), pp. 20-38.

Naik P.,A., & Raman K., (2003) Understanding the Impact of Synergy in Multimedia Communications. Journal of Marketing Research 40(4): 375–388.

Ortiz, M.H. and Harrison, M.P., 2011. Crazy Little Thing Called Love: A Consumer-Retailer Relationship. Journal of Marketing Development and Competitiveness, 5(3), pp. 68-80.

Patterson, M. and O'Malley, L., 2006. Brand, Consumers and Relationships: A Review. Irish Marketing Review, 18(1/2), pp. 10-20.

Peltier J.,W., Schibrowsky J.,A., & Schultz D.,E., (2003) Interactive Integrated Marketing Communication: Combining the Power of IMC, New Media and Database Marketing. International Journal of Advertising 22(1): 93–115.

Phipps, B., 2011. Brand strategy: Create your entire brand as a customer-focused application. Brands create customers, [blog] 1 March. Available at: http://tenayagroup.com/blog/2011/03/01/brand- strategy-create-your-entire-brand-as-a-customer-focused-application-2/ [Accessed 3 February,2018].

realitytechnologies.com (2018), The ultimate guide to understanding AR Technology, accessed 20 February, 2018.

Reid M., (2005) Performance Auditing of Integrated Marketing Communication (IMC) Actions and Outcomes. Journal of Advertising 34(4): 41–54.

Renner, C., 2013. Targeting soon – no longer allowed? Absatzwirtschaft.

Roberts., J., (2018) Different types of Mobile Payments Explained, mobiletransaction.com, accessed 31 May, 2018.

Rogers E.,M., (1986) Communication Technology: The New Media in Society. New York, NY: Free Press.

Rogers G., & Bouey E., (1996) Collecting Your Data. In: Tutty LM, Rothery R & Grinnell M Jr. (eds) Qualitative Research for Social Workers: Phases, Steps, and Tasks (4th edition) Boston, MA: Ally & Bacon: 50–87.

Rouse, M., Tech Target's IT encyclopaedia, WhatIs.com Accessed 3 February,2018

Rowley, J., 2004b. Online branding with McDonald's. British Food Journal, 106(3), pp. 228 – 237.

Salesforce.com, Inc., 2014. 2014 Mobile Behavior Report [pdf] salesforce.com, Inc. Available at: <http://www.exacttarget.com/sites/exacttarget/files/deliverables/etmc-2014mobilebehaviorreport.pdf> [Accessed 3 February 2018].

Samuelsson M., & Dholakia N., (2003) Assessing the Market Potential of Network-enabled 3G M-Business Services. In: Nansi S (ed) Wireless Communications and Mobile Commerce. Hershey, PA: Idea Group Publishing USA.

Schultz D.,E., (2002) Summit Explores Where IMC, CRM meet. Marketing News 36(5): 11– 12.

Seligman, J, (2018) Mobile Value Drivers, Research Gate Paper

Seligman, J., (2017) Mobile Marketing, Research Gate.

Shankar, V., and Hollinger, M., (2007) Online and Mobile Advertising, Research Gate.

Shankar, V., O'Driscoll, T., and Reibstein, D., (2003) Rational Exuberance: The Wireless Industry's Killer "B", Research Gate, accessed 3 February, 2018

Shimp T.,A., (2000) Advertising Promotion: Supplemental Aspects of Integrated Marketing Communications (5th edition). Fort Worth, TX: The Dryden Press, Harcourt College Publishers.

Stewart D.,W., & Pavlou P.,A., (2002) From Consumer Response to Active Consumer: Measuring the Effectiveness of Interactive Media. Journal of the Academy of Marketing Science 30(4): 376–396.

Textmarketer.co.uk 920170 Examples of SMs Marketing Messages, accesses 3 February,2017.

theappsolutions.com, (2018) Why is a Retail App useful for Business, accessed 8 February, 2018.

Veloutsou, C., Saren, M. and Tzokas, N., 2002. Relationship Marketing: What if...? European Journal of Marketing, 36(4), pp. 433-449.

Willis, K., S., 2009 A comparison of spatial knowledge acquisition with maps, and mobile maps, Computers, Environment and Urban Systems. Volume 33, Issue 2, March 2009, Pages 100-110.

Winer, R.S., 2009. New Communications Approaches in Marketing: Issues and Research Directions. Journal of Interactive Marketing, 23(2), pp. 108–117.

www. statistica,com. 2018.

www. wikipedia.Com, 2018.

www.techcrunch.com, 2018.

www.techradar, 2018.

www.TMR Direct, 2018.

Yadav M.,S., & Varadarajan R., (2005) Interactivity in the Electronic Marketplace: An Exposition of the Concept and Implications for Research. Journal of Academy of Marketing Science 33(4): 585–603.

Zincdigital.com (2018), The importance of Mobile Optimized Website in 2018, accessed 20 February,2018.

Zukunfts Intstitut, 2012. Megatrend Documentation. Available at: <http://www.zukunftsinstitut.de/artikel/megatrend-documentation/> [Accessed 6 February 2018].